FLO WER PAL ETTES

Stephen Woodhams

arranging flowers
using color as
your guide

photography by Lorry Eason

Clarkson Potter/Publishers
New York

Published by Clarkson N. Potter/Publishers, 201 East 50th Street,
New York, New York 10022. Member of the Crown Publishing Group.

Random House, Inc. New York, Toronto, London, Sydney, Auckland.
www.randomhouse.com

CLARKSON N. POTTER, POTTER, and colophon are trademarks of
Clarkson N. Potter, Inc.

Originally published in Great Britain by Quadrille Publishing Limited
in 1998.

Printed in Singapore

Library of Congress Cataloging-in-Publication Data
Woodhams, Stephen.
    Flower palettes: arranging flowers using color as your
guide/Stephen Woodhams; photography by Lorry Eason.–– 1st ed.
        p.   cm.
    Includes index.

    1. Flower arrangement.   2.Flowers––color.   I. Title.
SB449.W67 1998
745.92––dc21   98–28775
ISBN 0-609-60363-9   CIP
10 9 8 7 6 5 4 3 2 1
First American Edition

contents

dedicated to the one I love

Flowers are what I really love best so, in a way, this book is dedicated to them for all the joy they have brought me. I feel truly lucky to be thinking about and working with flowers all day long. They can do so many things. They can set the scene for a celebration; they can be a way of saying "I love you," "Thank you," or "I'm sorry"; or they can simply just be there to lift the spirits. Sometimes, if I'm having a dinner party and I'm in a panic about the food or who should sit where, I find that arranging the flowers for the table is a great way to relax. Or, when I get home after a hard day, just arranging a few flowers for myself in a favorite vase quickly enables me to unwind.

Being a floral decorator is not the easiest occupation in the world. I have to work very long hours, starting at the flower market at three in the morning, and often helping to put the final finishing touches to the flowers for a party at four in the afternoon—thirteen hours later! But even though I am now running a large business and have a wonderful team of people to help and support me in my relentless search for perfection and in my love of all things natural, I still feel there is no substitute for choosing my own flowers. It gives me the chance to make last-minute, perhaps unexpected combinations, and the end result is so rewarding that even after ten years, I find it just as exciting as when I began.

Another exciting aspect of being in this business is the opportunity to meet so many people who share my passion for flowers. Then there's the chance to add my own artistic statement to what are often stunningly aesthetic locations in their own right—great old houses, beautiful churches or chapels, magnificent banqueting halls or slickly contemporary convention centers.

Because of my other passion—for good food—some of my best experiences have been working with great chefs in their restaurants. Like a good meal, a good flower arrangement should leave you feeling happy and satisfied. In fact, that's not the only similarity so I like to follow the example of a friend who also happens to be a brilliant London chef. She firmly believes that foods are at their best when in season, so would never use strawberries except in June and July, or serve asparagus except in May, or raspberries except in August, or apples except in September and October. It's the same with my flower arranging. I try to stick to what's in season, avoiding tulips until February, roses until summer, and berries until the fall. Go with nature and the chances are, you will rarely get it wrong.

Ultimately, I hope, through this book to share with you my passion for flowers, a passion that I attribute to my grandfather, who was a nurseryman. Like me, he realized that one of the great things about flowers is that they do not recognize any class distinctions. Even the simplest ones can bring joy to our lives, whatever our background. I hope, too, that by reading this book, you will gain some ideas and confidence to help you arrange your flowers in a way that you can be proud of. But more than anything, I hope you will have as much fun with flowers as I do.

up, up, & away

the fundamentals of flower arranging

Have you ever bought some flowers that caught your eye and put them in your favorite vase in the living room, only to find that they just didn't look as good as you expected? Or seen a terrific container at a friend's, bought the same one, brought it home, and found that it looked truly awful?

The reason for these sometimes expensive mistakes is that every room, every container, even every flower, has its own character. A successful arrangement will be one that brings together those elements that have similar characters—though, if you are lucky enough to have an eye for them, unexpected combinations can be the most successful of all. Color, of course, is the other main element in an arrangement, so it's also important to know how colors affect one another. With a bit of practice, you'll soon get a feel for which combinations work.

Finally, in addition to giving some tips on the mechanics of flower arranging, I can't resist recommending my favorite flowers, foliage, and plants—tomorrow's classics. Some of these are just so fabulous that, to my mind, they will go on looking great and being chosen for flower arranging for many years to come.

good vibrations

What is it that makes some flower arrangements work and give out good vibrations, while others simply miss the mark? Most of us can look at an arrangement and immediately know if it's successful or not, if it makes the impact that's intended. But not all arrangements succeed. Although some people have an instinctive flair for flower arranging, most of the greatest arrangements haven't happened by chance. They've been worked on long and hard. Their success has a lot to do with the sensitive combination of the style of the flowers with their setting—more of that later—but the first impact of an arrangement is usually made by its color.

I am passionate about color. It's such an important part of our lives. Anyone is sure to remember the impact of an all-red arrangement in an all-white room, or the brightness that a crate of sunflowers will bring to a summer garden-party table, or the clarity of a white calla lily—even though white is not, strictly speaking, a color but an amalgam of all the colors of the rainbow.

Color preferences are very personal, and what one person likes, another could absolutely loathe. This is due partly to the way we associate different things with different colors. Some of us think of green as the color of the countryside and of soothing nature, while others associate it with the greens they had to eat as a child. For certain people, blue suggests the sky and the sea. I sometimes associate it with the color of my hated math textbook. Red can bring to mind drama and passion, or it can conjure up blood and carnage, while yellow might recall happy memories of childhood seaside vacations with sunshine and sand or the ghastly faded yellow paintwork of one's first rented apartment.

All these single colors are fairly straightforward, but things really get interesting when we start putting different colors next to one another, and that's where a bit of technical know-how doesn't come amiss. Basically, besides the three primary colors—red, blue, and yellow—the spectrum includes three secondaries—green, orange, and violet—as well as all the shades in between. Some of the colors of the spectrum are warm, and some are cool. We usually think of blues and greens as cool, and of reds and yellows as warm, but there are plenty of blues that veer toward purple and so have a touch of warmth about them, just as there are plenty of acid-yellows that are very definitely on the cool side, thanks to the bit of green in their make-up.

If you are looking for a harmonious color scheme, whether it's in choosing clothes, for a flower arrangement or for decorating a

room, the trick is to put together colors of approximately the same temperature. A cool harmony, for instance, that will make you feel relaxed and calm, could be made up of clear minty greens, gray-greens, and acid greens. For a summer wedding table centerpiece, I might make a container of green apples filled with lush green and gray-green foliage, clumps of lady's mantle, cream stocks, and lilies. All-foliage arrangements can also make cool harmonies, with the differing shapes and textures of the leaves adding to the effect, while clear, icy blues and mauves—combinations of lisianthus, irises, bachelor's buttons, love-in-a-mist, salvias, and thistles—are also great. For warm harmonies, go for reds, oranges, and yellows—amaryllis, crocosmia (also called montbretia), dahlias, roses, rudbeckias, gladioli, ornamental peppers—the list is endless. I must say that one of my favorite warm harmony combinations is made up of orange and yellow—the orange and yellow roses on page 50 or a mass of orange and yellow marigolds. Harmonies made up of these colors will be far from restful, but if you include cooled-down tints of reds, oranges, and yellows—pinks, pale oranges, and yellows—the effect will veer toward cool and calming again.

A sizzling combination of tulips in warm burgundy, yellow, and orange with cool purple will bring any room to life with its powerful intensity of color.

What beats the pizzazz of purple and orange? What packs more of a punch than turquoise and tangerine? What stops you in your tracks if not red and green? For drama like this in your flower arrangements, contrasts are a must.

A contrast is made when two complementary colors are put next to one another. On the color wheel—a visual aid often used for classifying color—complementary colors stand opposite one another. Since the color wheel also has warm and cool colors opposite one another, a true contrast will be a contrast of temperature as well as one of color. Put two complementaries next to each other, and for somewhat technical reasons, each will enhance the effect of the other. So in a combination of orange gerberas with lime-green lady's mantle, the orange will look even more orange and the lime-green more strongly green. That's part of what makes contrasts so powerful.

BELOW

The combination of a hot red nerine and a bright orange vase is almost unbearable, while Nature makes its own dramatic contrast with a red and white x *Vuylstekeara* cambria orchid.

To make the process more complicated, you can also have contrasts of tone—the lightness or darkness of a color. Think of deep purple violas and pale narcissi, for example. Or deep purple heuchera with pale green bells of Ireland. White gives the most intense contrasts of tone with any color, simply because nothing comes paler than white, but strangely enough, the strongest contrasts actually come from colors that are closest in tone—somehow the closeness of tone emphasizes the color difference even more. The red berries of holly contrast brilliantly with the green of its foliage. Clear red geraniums sing out against their bright green leaves.

wild thing

Then there are the color contrasts that shock with their audacity. Scarlet, pink, and orange. Purple, orange, and blue. Purple, orange, and red. Their strength comes from the fact that they seem to be harmonious mixes of colors, but in fact, they use colors of different temperatures. This temperature combination causes a powerful clash, like a warm and cold front creating a thunderstorm. Purple lisianthus will set white flowers alight, but put the cool lisianthus with warm red or orange gerberas, and you'll get a real conflagration. Cool blue and white flowers make a classic combination, but add hot purple and orange for maximum vibrancy. The heat is on!

come together

In my work as a professional designer, the starting point for most of my flower arrangements or installations is usually a specific location, often with a particular occasion in mind. For instance, I might be asked to do the flowers for a society wedding, for a gathering of politicians at a convention center, or for a dear friend's birthday party. Certain locations and occasions usually suggest a specific style, mood, or atmosphere. A bunch of flowers laid in a wooden basket that look as if they have been freshly picked from the yard would not be appropriate to grace the table at a gathering of businessmen, nor would a single stem of the bold, graphic lobster claws look good in a cozy, beamed living room in the depths of the country.

Broadly speaking, styles of arrangements fall into just three categories—the country look, the classic look, and contemporary, or urban, chic. Formality and informality are factors to be taken into account, too. Nowadays informality holds sway. We see far less of the stiffly formal style of flower arranging that was common in the 1970s and '80s. That is obvious even in the way florists make up bouquets today. Now they are often presented hand-tied and wrapped in brown paper or clear cellophane, sometimes with a piece of colored tissue paper as well. Gone, thank heavens, are those huge, ugly, flat bouquets that look more suitable for laying on a coffin than for giving as a birthday present or as a gift to celebrate the birth of a child.

Often there is some overlap between the different styles and

formality and informality. For example, if I put a mass of single-colored wallflowers—a typical cottage-garden flower—into a galvanized pot, they become unexpectedly contemporary, more so if I have cut them all to the same length. What is normally seen as an informal, loose-looking, country-style flower is suddenly given a modern twist. In a similar vein, if I combine calla lilies—one of the great classics of the flower world—with some vivid green stems of bamboo and finish them off with a collar of anthurium leaves around the neck of the vase, I will have created something rather startling. It is this element of the unexpected that is so much a feature of my flower arranging and that gives it, I think, its modern edge. It is also what makes choosing and arranging flowers so exciting for me.

For most people, either the flowers they grow in their yard or the ones they can buy from their local florist will be the starting point and can dictate the style of an arrangement. You might go out to buy stately lilies, but return with a homey bunch of anemones. To my mind, flowers with a rounded, loose appearance, such as roses, sweet peas, campanulas, scabious, bachelor's buttons, poppies, and peonies, have an informal, country feel to them. For a formal, modern look, I would choose strongly graphic, often spiky or abstract-looking flowers or foliage—irises, globe artichokes, bells of Ireland, amaryllis, gladioli, calla lilies, lobster claws, agapanthus, gerberas, strelitzias, or snapdragons (another cottage-garden flower but now commercially produced to make a flower with stronger, more graphic lines than the garden-grown specimens.) These architectural plants and flowers usually look

Don't go for the obvious. The owner of this house was expecting a formal arrangement of roses, lilies, and foliage for the console table in the hall. Instead, I chose the more audacious alternative of stripes of orange and yellow roses in a rough wooden tray.

best on their own, or with only one other type of flower or foliage. In fact, it is generally true that varieties used by themselves will look more contemporary, while mixtures are more traditional looking.

But these are not hard and fast rules. A flower can suggest many different things, depending on the way it is used. Take roses, for instance. Usually they are associated with the countryside, romance, and informality. You only have to look at the straw hat garlanded with large, blowsy roses on page 138 to see what I mean. But change to commercially grown roses, with their small, evenly matched heads and their stems all the same length, put them in a plain, frosted glass vase in an urban living room, and you have an undeniable example of contemporary urban chic. Similarly, lilies used on their own look very crisp and modern, but mixed with other flowers, they add a touch of classicism to any arrangement. Delphiniums are another example. Usually thought of as a traditional cottage-garden plant, they take on a crisp, modern look when massed together in shades of blue (see page 64). Mixed with white flowers, they have a classic feel, while in a mixed arrangement with other cottage-garden flowers, they project a country image. Foxtail lilies are similar. Combined with other flowers in a huge urn (see page 52), they look very classic, but on their own, with just a few big leaves, they become unexpectedly modern and very urban.

Your choice of container is another important factor. You should possess as big a selection as possible, as the container can make all the difference to a design. The bold flowers that suit contemporary interiors will make the main statement, so here the container should be plain and simple, so there is no vying for attention. Try a mass of huge white agapanthus in a clear glass vase with bold swiss cheese leaves (see page 120), or a single paphiopedilum orchid in a clear glass bowl, or a white phalenopsis orchid (also called a moth orchid) with a stem of Hankow willow in a creamware pot. Another stunning idea for a contemporary urban environment would be a mass of white tulips—among my favorite flowers—in a simple green vase, or white gerberas in frosted glass (see page 113). Contemporary locations also suit industrial-looking containers, such as concrete blocks (see page 84), metal rods lined with blown glass (see page 82), or test tubes, either used singly (see page 92) or linked together in a metal frame (see pages 46 and 134).

For traditional arrangements, go for the classic, rounded shapes of urns, in glass, metal, porcelain, or stone—a tall, frosted goblet-shaped vase filled with romantic summer flowers in harmonizing shades (see page 100), or a glass urn filled with tightly packed heads of a single type of rose, without any foliage except, perhaps, a collar of leaves around the neck of the vase—or for vases made

Containers come in enormous variety. Old pewter jugs are full of character and look great even without any flowers. So does the simple nickel-plated vase. It is almost a work of art in its own right. The wooden crate filled with lupines and the pair of creamware pots make a totally different kind of statement.

My vase collection is continually growing. I have lots of favorites, though I must say these can change from season to season, depending on the flowers I am working with. It's always nice to see their stems through clear glass, but the disadvantage, of course, is that as soon as the water gets murky, it shows. When that happens, change it. It's better for the flowers and for the aesthetic sense, too.

The bold simplicity of a handful
of yellow calla lilies in a plain
glass vase complements the
abstract painting in the
background.

of creamware, another design classic that is making a comeback. Pottery pitchers, pewter, colored glass, and baskets all make good containers for country-style arrangements, and don't forget the possibilities of simple wooden trugs or crates for informal arrangements of cut flowers or plants (see pages 42, 55, and 111).

Once you have a good collection of containers, you will quickly realize that some of them can be used in a variety of ways. A glass salad bowl could, when not needed for salad, be used for flower arrangements. Place a ring of florist's foam around the top, and stud it with flowers, candles, and foliage, then fill the center with water and votive candles (see page 130). You can use the same container with an inner, plastic bowl. Line the space between the glass and the plastic with orange slices and vivid green moss, and fill the plastic bowl with a mass of harmonizing flowers. Another idea is to line the glass bowl with whole lemons, and plant the plastic bowl with yellow Persian ranunculus, or to line it with pebbles, lichen, and driftwood and to place a smaller glass bowl in the center filled with red anemones and small cherry tomatoes. Now we're back to salad again!

Ultimately, when you bring everything together, you must come back to your room setting. A wood-paneled dining room could be crying out for a classical metal urn filled with assorted flowers and foliage in the style of an old Dutch still-life painting. These old paintings aimed to show the widest possible variety of fruits and flowers, somewhat like botanical records, regardless of whether or not they were all in season at the same time. This effect is relatively easy to emulate nowadays, when so many fruits and flowers are available in stores for twelve months of the year. To achieve this look, I would choose stately flowers such as crown imperials, Parrot tulips, and 'Stargazer' lilies and mix them with the more country-style old-fashioned pinks, purple lilac, foxgloves, peonies, and clusters of roses. Then I would wire some grapes into the front of the arrangement and would strew cascades of apples, pears, and more grapes around the foot of the urn.

As a complete contrast, the most breathtaking addition to a minimalist living room, containing nothing more than a couple of sofas, a coffee table, and a huge, abstract painting, might be just a plain glass vase of yellow calla lilies, their curvy stems tied with a piece of raffia, to create a perfect echo of the painting behind. What could be more simple, yet more beautiful and more appropriate?

The exquisite texture and color of this rusty urn in a classic shape work so well with the flowers and ornaments on the mantelpiece that they seem made for each other. The mellow, aged look of the urn adds to the elegance of the setting.

a little help from my friends

Loose, arching stems of sotol in a narrow-necked vase almost look like a crazy hairstyle gone mad. They will add an exciting sense of movement to any arrangement.

foliage & berries

Having trained as a gardener, I feel very strongly about foliage. I was always taught that, in garden design, the key features, apart from the hard landscaping, are the trees and shrubs. These form the backdrop to the flowers. I like to think of my flower arrangements in the same way, and unless an arrangement is to be very minimalist, I usually start with at least three different types of foliage. The choice is not as narrow as you might think, and many can easily be grown in your own yard.

For an arrangement of strong, bold colors, I use dark green foliage as a counterbalance. Some of my favorites are *Viburnum tinus*, myrtle, Mexican orange, and camellia. For white flowers, which might be overwhelmed by strong greens, choose variegated foliage such as pittosporum, or lime-green types— for example, *Euphorbia polychroma*. For pinks and blues, nothing looks better than foliage from the silver-gray palette. Here the variety is wide. Try whitebeam (also known as mountain ash), or one of the many varieties of eucalyptus. One of my favorite foliage plants is *Brachyglottis* 'Sunshine,' which has silver-gray leaves with a white margin and underside. I also like to use rosemary and the silvery spider's web-type leaves of the globe artichoke. If you are working with rich burnt oranges and yellows, go for foliage with the same warmth of color. Choose copper beech, smoke tree, or berries such as ash, or *Viburnum tinus*. Another unusual choice would be the beautiful arching seed heads of crocosmia.

Certain berries and foliage are my first choice in special situations. The burgundy-red berries of hypericum, for example, make a superb base for a hand-tied bouquet in shades of red. I love using ivy, too, not only when I need some trailing strands in an arrangement, but also for its individual leaves, which look great with votive candles standing on top for a party. For a contemporary tablescape, I often use banana leaves cut into geometric shapes and placed beneath sections of bamboo stems to make candle-holders. Exquisitely aromatic laurel leaves are great glued around a plastic pot, for lining glass dishes, or with winter foliage in a Christmas arrangement. Dried, it can be used for a kitchen display with a culinary theme.

Grasses, like the vivid green sotol, are becoming ever more popular. Their graphic simplicity makes them ideal for contemporary arrangements. I also love using papyrus heads submerged in water, or fresh wheat with its blue plumes. The water-loving horsetail is another star. You can make containers out of it, use it to add a touch of originality to a hand-tied bouquet, or use it as a decorative support for flowering plants. Finally, tropical plants, many of them introduced into Europe in the nineteenth century, are being used more and more today. Their highly graphic appearance means that they usually look best on their own. One of my favorites is the swiss cheese plant. Its dramatic foliage is so unusual, it's hard to believe it's real.

plants

Because they are long-lasting, I use plants in arrangements whenever I can. They also give me the opportunity to do something a bit different. Once I stumbled across a crate of lupines in mixed colors awaiting delivery at a nursery. They looked so wonderful, I couldn't think of anything better than copying the idea, so I planted a mass of them in a plastic-lined crate as a centerpiece for a summer buffet table. I also get a thrill from watching bulbs slowly come into bloom. Stately amaryllis, available mostly in red, pink, and white, are such good value. They look great in a modern container or in a rustic wooden box, and they last well. They are terrific as their tall, chunky stems reach for the sky and their fat flower buds slowly unfurl into wonderful, exotic-looking flowers. Hyacinths are very versatile, too, and have the bonus of their wonderful scent. For an arrangement with urban chic, I would fill a low, galvanized dish with white hyacinth bulbs, but for a country look, I would plant them in a plain wooden container with fine grass growing on top. In fact, grass is another useful plant. Nothing looks more funky than a shallow wooden box lined with plastic

Mosses and lichens are a must. I sometimes use them by themselves, but usually as extras. Different types of moss lend themselves to different situations. To make a moss garland to disguise an otherwise ordinary container, I use shaggy, green sphagnum moss. The compact look of bun moss is great for top-dressing a planted arrangement, while gray, spongelike lichen suits contemporary compositions, especially in galvanized containers. For an arrangement with a tropical feel, I would usually choose Spanish moss, which is gray with a shredded, hairlike texture.

I love using growing plants in my arrangements. For one thing, they last a lot longer than cut flowers, and for another, there is the fun of watching them grow. Ivy is not a fussy plant and will often grow in poor light, where other plants would simply give up and die. It looks especially good trained around a frame to make an indoor topiary. Here I have combined it with some thick twigs for extra interest.

and filled with a piece of cultivated turf. This "grass panel" would be great in a minimalist interior, as would one made of sprouting grains of wheat. These come up such a vivid green and last about a week indoors.

Orchids are classic plants, but don't just display them in the pot they come in. Phalenopsis orchids are wonderful, either in old terracotta, creamware, or galvanized pots or in glass containers, perhaps with silver sand and shells to give them a nautical theme. x *Vuylstekeara* cambria orchids, especially the wonderful burgundy and white or yellow and brown forms, are also great favorites of mine. The yellow and brown ones have a truly autumnal feel when planted in a Lucite container lined with wheat.

Cacti are becoming increasingly popular now, and come in a wider range of sizes than before. They work well in contemporary, minimalist locations and need very little maintenance, which makes them a good buy for people with busy lives. If you are looking for larger, structural plants, some of the cacti will fit the bill, or I would recommend the plaited-stem weeping fig.

Topiary trees add yet another range of possibilities. Choose from standard rosemary, olive, azalea, or *Magnolia stellata* trees, all of which, although usually grown outdoors, can be brought inside for a while. Don't forget, too, the possibilities of ivy topiaries. These can be trained as standard trees, pyramids, globes, or basket shapes. They are rather expensive to buy because of all the care that has gone into them, but they are not difficult to train yourself.

A few other favorites of mine include the 1960s-style money plant, growing in a glass dish with pebbles. Like baby's tears, this is a very clean-cut plant which makes a strong impact in any room. And finally, don't forget plants that not only flower but have beautiful leaves. The peace lily is one of these. It looks stunning, showing off its dark green leaves and white sails for almost twelve months of the year.

dried flowers

Dried flowers are no longer relegated to some dusty corner of a country cottage. The choice of dried material is better now than it has ever been, and this has helped to bring dried arrangements to the forefront of flower arranging. Drying methods now include freeze-drying at many degrees below zero. This keeps the natural bright colors of the flowers and fruit, and when they are used in arrangements, they take back some moisture from the air, which gives them a very lifelike appearance.

Instead of using an old-fashioned jumble of dried flowers, the contemporary approach is to use a mass of one flower—domes of dried roses in simple containers, plain glass vases filled with potpourri and topped with dried lavender heads, stems of lavender edged with red roses, or different shades of pink and red peonies in old terracotta pots. For a contemporary kitchen, I would line a glass container with dried peas, and top it off with a dome of ears of dried wheat. Or a rustic panel of woven twigs would look great with a collection of old terracotta pots wired on, together with a few wooden kitchen utensils and some dried herbs.

Dried-flower mirror frames are another of my favorites. Those made of a mass of dried, assorted flowers (see page 126) remind me of the work of Grinling Gibbons, that master of late seventeenth- and early eighteenth-century woodcarving. They would suit a classic interior. For contemporary appeal, though, you can't beat a mirror edged with tufts of bun moss or, for the bathroom, try a mirror edged with glued-on shells accompanied by wired-in creamware pots filled with phalenopsis orchids.

Sculptured trees are another use for dried material. Use stems of silver birch or bamboo poles, to which you attach florist's foam studded with bun moss, dried box, heads of dried flowers, or even dried palm leaves. For a modern twist, I sometimes wrap the stems of these trees in steel cable. "Cloud trees" (see pages 68-9), with their oriental feel, are similar to sculptured trees. Their "suspended" clusters of flowerheads or moss resemble clouds in the sky. Both these types of "tree" have something of the quality of a piece of art.

For long-lasting arrangements, you should follow a few simple tips. First, give your flowers and foliage a good deep drink of clean water, preferably overnight, removing all the lower leaves so they do not start rotting. Wrap long, floppy-stemmed plants like tulips and gerberas in paper first to help prevent them from bending.

Certain stems need to be specially treated. Woody stems used to be crushed with a hammer, but it is now thought that this does more harm than good because it makes the stems susceptible to bacterial attack. Instead, cut them at a 45-degree angle, to expose the largest possible surface area to the water. Hollow-stemmed plants like amaryllis have a tendency to collapse. To prevent this, run thin canes up the stems, fill with water, plug them with absorbent cotton, and secure at the end with a rubber band. I use a lot of spurge in my flower arranging, but they ooze a white liquid from their stems every time they are cut. Before you put them in an arrangement, leave them standing in a bucket of water so the milky liquid runs out; otherwise, they will make the water cloudy. Many other soft-stemmed plants, such as poppies, can be prevented from wilting if their stems are sealed, either by singeing with a naked flame or by holding them in shallow boiling water for a few seconds. First wrap the flowers up in stiff paper to protect them from the steam. Roses also last longer if they have their stems immersed in boiling water for a few seconds.

Whenever possible, I try to arrange my flower displays in fresh water, as they last longer than in wet florist's foam. Sometimes this is not practical, though—for example, in an arrangement for a wall-hanging or a pew-end in a church. For these, I try to use mostly woody-stemmed plants that hold up well in foam, rather than fleshy-stemmed plants like hyacinths.

Next, we come to the arrangement itself. The base of a classic arrangement is the foliage. It gives the shape, so it is hugely important, and I would always use at least three different varieties. Sometimes I end up with five or more, then I might think that to add flowers would spoil it, so I end up making another composition for the flowers! Lilies are a must for a classic arrangement, and they should follow the foliage. After that, add the spiky flowers and then the fillers placed in drifts of odd numbers—three, five or seven stems at a time. Finally I add clusters of my "star performers"—round-headed flowers like roses, gerberas, or peonies. The finished result should look like a section of an herbaceous border, with its interesting color mixes and variety of shape and form. Modern, graphic designs need a different approach, of course, but I still stick to using odd numbers of flowers and foliage.

help!

For some designs, you need to use wiring. This can range from something as simple as chicken wire to support large, heavy stems, to the individual wiring-up of fruits or vegetables (see page 48). Often, if I am making an arrangement of flowering plants, I finish it off with tufts of bun moss pinned down with hairpin-shaped wires. Wiring really comes into its own at Christmas, when nearly everything is wired—clumps of blue spruce, fir cones, and walnuts—often helped by a little dab of glue for extra support. I'll wire flowers only as a desperate last resort, though. For instance, if a gerbera insists on bending, I might insert a wire into the back of its head and wrap it around the stem, but on the whole I believe that flowers should be left to do their own thing and not be messed around with.

One very artificial type of flower arrangement is the sculptured tree. For this you will need to cement the stem or stems into a plastic pot, then fit it into the final display pot. If you try cementing the stem into a porcelain pot, as the cement dries it will expand and crack the porcelain. You should also make sure that any moss you use for these trees is completely dry, because if there is any moisture left in it, it will travel along the stems of any dried flowers you use, and make them rot.

Rose

Roses form a very large genus of around 125 species. Old garden roses are among my favorite flowers because of their shape and fragrance. Cultivated varieties are invaluable for their many useful colors. Some of these—for instance R. 'Ecstasy' and R. 'Jacaranda'—are fragrant, too.

Flowering prunus

These flowers always remind me of spring. Long before the leaves emerge, their blossom is the first sign of life after winter. The pale pink *Prunus* x *subhirtella* 'Autumnalis' can flower as early as December or January.

Flowering prunus

Nearly all the flowering prunus originated in Japan. They often appear in old Japanese prints and drawings.

Nerine

Named after Nerine, the water nymph, this beautiful flower originally came from South Africa. Its elegant flower heads, many from a central stem, are produced before the leaves. The hybrid varieties range from shades of pale pink and white to hot pinks, reds, lilacs, and purples.

tomorrow's classics

Belladonna lily

Related to the amaryllis, the belladonna lily is a bulb that is native to South Africa and usually flowers between August and October. Its rich, soapy smell is one of my favorite flower fragrances. It is mostly found in this stunning pink, but is also beautiful in white.

Bells of Ireland

This is a lovely annual which, although it can be problematic, may be grown from seed for the front of a border. In the garden it grows multistemmed, rather than with the single slender stems it has when grown commercially.

Bells of Ireland

This is one of my favorite green flowers, and works well on its own for a clean, modern look, or as part of a mixed arrangement. Spiky and structural, It also makes a good dried flower.

Gerbera

Named after the eighteenth-century German naturalist Traugott Gerber, the gerbera is wonderful, either by itself or as the highlight of a mixed arrangement. It is also great as a houseplant. Do not overwater, and it will produce flowers for months.

Gerbera

This dark burgundy—'Chateau'—variety, with its golden eye, is one of the most stunning. Among my other favorites are the bright orange 'Tennessee' and the golden yellow 'Dallas.'

...flowers

Lobster claws

These come from a family of tropical blooms from South America. They are very bold and dramatic, great for a minimalist treatment, as well as with a mass of other flowers. One of my favorites, with its red and yellow hanging flowers is *Heliconia rosrata*.

Hyacinth

There are around 30 species of hyacinth, a plant named after Hyacinthus, lover of Apollo. When Hyacinthus was killed, hyacinths were said to spring from his blood. As a cut flower, it brings definition and a glorious scent to any arrangement.

Tulip

This is a very early variety of plant, first brought to Europe from Constantinople in 1562. Now, almost 4,000 horticultural varieties have been developed. With its wide range of colors—almost every shade except true blue—and forms, it is one of the most popular flowers.

Spurge

This is another green flower, to add a touch of the vividly unexpected to an arrangement. To my mind, the best variety is *Euphorbia characias* subsp. *wulfenii*, a perennial with bluish-green leaves and nodding flowers. *E. polychroma* comes a close second.

Gladiolus

This is a genus of more than 150 species which flower in late summer. Fashionable about 30 years ago, their time has, I think, come again. Nothing beats a mass of single-color stems in a vase, and they last well as cut flowers, too.

Lilac

Most common in white or lilac color, lilac usually has a lovely subtle fragrance. Unfortunately, it does not last long once cut, and many people are suspicious about having it indoors as it is sometimes thought to bring bad luck.

Guelder rose

This most wonderful shrub is a must for any flower-lover's garden. As its acid-green flowers grow, they develop into puffy, creamy-white balls. In the fall the shrub becomes a mass of red berries and terrific rich, vibrant red foliage.

Tuberose

Tuberoses have most amazing creamy-white flowers, often tinged with pink, and a heavy, rich scent. They grow only in warm climates, so are often imported and therefore expensive to buy and, unfortunately, do not last well when cut. But they are worth it.

Guelder rose

Although the flowers of the guelder rose look good with almost anything, they are especially spectacular combined with purple and orange.

Aspidistra

This was very popular as a houseplant in the nineteenth century, but I like to use it for its bold architectural foliage, folded around the edge of a hand-tied bouquet, or submerged in water, in a clear glass vase. It lasts extremely well.

Dogwood

This is a shrub whose bare winter stems have many uses. I like the red *Cornus alba* at Christmas, mixed with other winter foliage, wrapped around containers, or for staking amaryllis. I also use the pale greenish-yellow *C. stolonifera* 'Flaviramea' to wrap the stems of dried-flower trees.

Flowering eucalyptus

This is a very useful Australian foliage. I use shorter lengths of flowering eucalyptus (*E. perriniana*) in hand-tied bouquets, or as a base for table decorations. Longer stems are ideal in large urns. Other varieties are useful, too—the large round leaves of *E. gunnii*, and feathery *E. parvifolia*.

Garrya elliptica

This is another great garden shrub, for a south- or west-facing wall. In early winter It bears amazing silver-green catkins that add an air of mystery and sense of movement to any composition, whether it be an arrangement or a hand-tied bouquet.

tomorrow's classics

Horsetail

This is a foliage with many uses. Dress up a container with stems of horsetail glued to the outside. Submerge it in water in a glass, so the fascinating stems are magnified. Split it and use to cover stakes to support a flowering orchid.

Brachyglottis 'Sunshine'

This silvery-gray evergreen has got to be one of my all-time favorites, both in the garden and for flower arranging. It adds an English country feel to whatever you mix it with and looks especially good in all-white compositions.

Magnolia grandiflora

This plant is a real garden favorite of mine. Beautiful just as it is, or grown as a large-leafed topiary tree, or against a wall, its glossy evergreen leaves have a wonderful textured suede underside. Dried, they can be used to make sculptured trees.

Photinia 'Red Robin'

This is another excellent garden shrub whose new spring leaves are a beautiful bronze-red color. It makes a stunningly opulent composition with other reds and purples. Once the foliage has matured and turned a rich green, I still find it very useful as a base foliage.

Sotol

This native of Texas and the Mexican highlands is useful for its delicate, loose habit. I like to use it in hand-tied bouquets, especially wedding bouquets. It also works well in more graphic arrangements.

...foliage

Fan palm

Palm leaves are a must for a tropical arrangement, even as an edging for a tropical hand-tied bouquet. They are great, too, laid flat on a table as a base for a display of tropical fruit. They will dry quickly if you leave them out of water. Try them sprayed gold for Christmas.

Galax

This useful plant, native to eastern North America, has evergreen leaves that often turn bronze in winter. They can last up to three weeks in water. I like to use them as an edging to a small hand-tied bouquet, and I sometimes wrap them around glass votive candles for an extra decorative touch.

Feathered papyrus

This is a lush green grasslike foliage with a tropical-marsh quality. For a tropical foliage arrangement, I mix it with anthurium leaves, fan palm, and clumps of horsetail. Stems all cut to the same length and tied together can make an unusual ball shape, like an oriental-style topiary.

Anthurium

This very distinctive, heart-shaped, dark green glossy leaf lasts well in water. I love to use them as a bold defining collar around the edge of a vase. Otherwise, a single leaf looks great with a stem of, say, amaryllis—a striking flower that can hold its own.

Cycas palm

This glossy dark green leaf has a very strong character. Only similarly strong flowers can stand up to it. I love combining it with bold white flowers such as amaryllis, or 'Casa Blanca' lilies.

Variegated pittosporum

Pittosporums are great garden shrubs, but since they are slow-growing, you are unlikely to want to cut them. Commercially grown large or small-leafed variegated varieties are available instead. They go with most color palettes, and their variegation will add sparkle to any arrangement.

Papyrus

This amazing plant bears an enormous profusion of grasslike tufts from its lush green fibrous stem. Added to any arrangement , it brings a strong sense of structure. On its own, with its tufts trimmed to the same length, it is unbeatable.

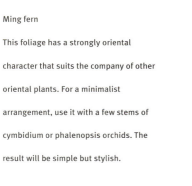

Ming fern

This foliage has a strongly oriental character that suits the company of other oriental plants. For a minimalist arrangement, use it with a few stems of cymbidium or phalenopsis orchids. The result will be simple but stylish.

Swiss cheese plant or Mexican breadfruit

This is one of the most distinctive leaf forms I have ever used. Its glossy green, deeply cut contours are effective as an edging to an arrangement or—my favorite—under water in a clear glass vase, to help disguise the stems of other flowers.

x *Vuylstekeara* cambria orchid

With its exotic, complex flower, this orchid can range from white to dark burgundy. Planted in a simple wooden container topped with bark chippings, it adds a dose of magically intense color, especially in a richly decorated dark-paneled room.

Paphiopedilum orchid

My favorite of these orchids is *P.* x Maudiae, this lovely green and white variety. The flower itself reminds me of a bumble bee—the very insect it is designed to attract for polination.

Hyacinth

One of the treats of including hyacinth bulbs in an arrangement is that you can watch them grow. Individual white hyacinths in creamware pots, each with a plant label giving the guest's name, look stunning for a wedding-party table setting.

Phalenoposis orchid

This is a classic of the orchid world whose arching stems, with—usually—white flowers, look best just on their own. It also comes in hot pink and cream. Because it doesn't like its roots being disturbed, take care when planting into your own container.

tomorrow's classics

Dendrobium orchid

This white dendrobium orchid is my favorite. Other stunners are 'Madame Pompadour'—a strking purple—and 'James Storey'—a dark orange-red, often used with fall foliage and winter evergreens.

Amaryllis

This is a stately, architectural bulb to grow yourself and brighten up the winter. At Christmas, I love red ones in dark wooden bowls or baskets. White looks good in galvanized or creamware pots, topped with gray lichen.

Jasmine

Jasmine is a classic plant that looks best on its own—for example, on a coffee table. For a traditional setting I might use it in a creamware pot supported by twigs of silver birch. For a contemporary location, simply spray the twigs with silver paint.

Ivy topiary

Ivy can be trained along wires to form different shapes—a solid ball, a hollow globe, or even an animal shape. Use small-leafed varieties, and preferably plain green, not variegated. They can be trained quite quickly—one season should give your shape—but watch out for insects.

'Tête-à-tête' narcissus

With its not-too-large blooms and long flowering period, this is one of the most commonly grown narcissi. I love to plant a mass of them in a glass container lined with gravel and topped with lush green bun moss. If they need staking, use birch twigs.

...plants

marmalade skies

I love the yellows. They range, from pale, delicate narcissi to golden bright forsythia, and from orange gourds and pumpkins, to

rusty lilies. Chinese witch hazel is one of my favorite plants, with its amazing fragrance and flowers like crinkled ribbon. The bonus

is its wonderful golden-yellow leaves in the fall. Cornelian cherry is another favorite, with small clusters of spiky yellow flowers on

its bare winter branches, while in summer, no matter where I am, the sight of sunflower fields always reminds me of Umbria in Italy.

LEFT, FROM TOP
Sunny-faced rudbeckias, bright
yellow narcissi, and the
greenish-yellow of the guelder
rose show how tones of yellow
makes a splash whatever the
time of year.

I often find it difficult to combine yellow flowers—especially the brighter ones—with other colors. In general, paler yellows, creamy yellows, or yellows with a hint of green are easier to work with. These combine well with each other, with green foliage, or with very pale blues or violets. The more difficult egg-yolk yellows or buttercup yellows have some red in them, so work best with reds and oranges. The yellow foliage of some of the grasses or yellow-variegated foliage also combine successfully with yellow flowers.

Solid yellow-white gerbera contrast with delicate sprays of lady's mantle. The colors of the variegated pittosporum pull all the yellows together. Lady's mantle, fresh or dried, is invaluable.

the freshness of spring

LEFT AND BELOW

For this arrangement, I used a
medium-weave rectangular
basket lined with a plastic bowl
filled with chicken wire. First I
made a base of berried ivy, and
of forsythia, hazel, and alder
catkins. Then I threaded
through long stems of white
Christmas roses. Displayed in
this basket, the flowers look as
if they have just been picked
from the yard.

BELOW

To make the smaller
arrangement, I put in a row of
forsythia, all cut to the same
height, then threaded the
Christmas roses through. I
especially love seeing the
stems of the flowers through
the frosted plastic.

Here, I wanted to show what can be done using the same flowers—forsythia and Christmas
roses—but in different ways. Christmas roses always remind me of my mother, as she is a great
collector of plants and grows them in her garden. They are truly wonderful, with their clusters of
nodding heads on long stems bringing a breath of life to an English garden during the cold winter
months. In addition to white, Christmas roses also come in a pale pink, burgundy, shades of green,
and even a yellow, so it is a very versatile plant for flower arrangers. The main arrangement here is
in traditional country-house style, but I have given it an interesting twist by putting this classic
in modern surroundings. The other arrangement, in a flat, narrow vase made of frosted plastic
and without the catkins, has a much more contemporary feel to it.

This arrangement happened more by accident than by design. When I bought the dried roses, I carried them home in the wooden crate. It was the first container I laid my hands on. Then I simply rearranged the roses slightly. The result is unexpectedly successful.

This is another example of what can be done using the same material, but in different ways. During the winter months, when the crate is not filled with sunflower plants (see page 55), I use it to show off several bunches of dried yellow roses. I have simply laid them in the crate in a casual, country manner. For a classic feel, pairs of creamware pots, like those above and opposite, look good placed on a mantelpiece, a dresser, or, as here, on an attractive old lamp table. The lamp adds a lovely finishing touch, casting its warm glow on the objects against the yellow wall. Pots like these also work very well in a contemporary location—say as a pair offset on a glass-topped coffee table, or on Lucite side tables with lamps on each side of a bed.

dried yellow roses

It is easy to fill creamware pots with dried roses like this. Just fill your pot with a round ball of florist's foam, leaving a third of the foam above the rim, then simply push the rose heads in, starting with the row closest to the rim. Continue row by row until you reach the center.

These golden shower orchids always remind me of miniature yellow butterflies: so delicate, yet so vibrant when the sun shines through them. Here I have used them in a bowl surrounded by my favorite honeycomb candles. The rich texture and color of the candles make an interesting and original combination with the copper wire wrapped around. To form the support that holds the candles, cut a piece of chicken wire deep enough to conceal the bowl and long enough to wrap around it several times. Attach it to the bowl with crisscrossed wire. To position the candles, push a piece of wire through each, twist its ends together, and use the twisted ends to wire the candles to the chicken-wire collar. The copper wire around the outside adds extra support and is a nice design detail, while the clusters of three small candles make a lovely finishing touch. With some care, orchids are long-lasting. Don't overwater, as they do not like to be sitting in moisture. Also, try to keep them out of direct sunlight. As the old flowers fade, new ones develop. If you are lucky, you might manage to persuade this variety of orchid to flower again the following year.

golden shower orchids

1

Make a chicken-wire collar and anchor it around the bowl. Wire in the candles, turning them upside down so the wicks do not show and they cannot be lit.

2

With the candles in place, wrap copper wire around the outside. Wire in bundles of three small candles around the circumference, using more copper wire.

3

Pot the orchids into the bowl using special orchid medium. I used three plants and left some of their roots showing to add to the effect.

4

Add bamboo stakes to support the orchids and for color coordination. Tie the stems to them with small pieces of copper wire.

5

Level off the medium, then dress it with grains of wheat, whose color links with that of the candles and the orchids. You can use moss or lichen instead.

The table is made of frosted glass with a clear glass center, and I used frosted and clear glassware at the place settings to echo this. The frosted glass picks up the color of the white narcissi, while the golden pine floorboards, seen through the center of the table, complement the yellow ones.

This test-tube snake is one of my favorite vases. It consists of a metal frame holding clear glass test tubes and can be bent to the shape you want. I have also used it to hold white nerines and papyrus (see page 134). Here, I have made the vase into a circle and placed it as a centerpiece on a circular dining table. The arrangement itself is very simple—nothing more than alternating clusters of 'Paper White' and 'Soleil d'Or' narcissi. As a final touch, I have positioned clear glass votive candles within the circle made by the vase. The light reflects through the water and stems and across the table in a particularly magical way.

Narcissi come in many guises, ranging from delicate single white flowers, through creamy doubles and the cyclamen-type with reflexed petals, to bright yellow trumpets. They are brilliant either as cut flowers or in the garden, and if you grow them indoors, you can plant them in the yard afterward to flower again the following year. Among my favorites are 'Paper White' narcissi, with their amazing fragrance and glistening white flowers, and 'Bridal Crown,' whose cream and orange semi-double flowers again have a beautiful scent and last well as cut flowers.

narcissi

The linear quality of this minimalist white interior lends itself to the simple, clear glass vase and the succulent, thick stems of the narcissi. I packed in as many stems as possible to produce a substantial, compact head of flowers. As a focal point at the end of a limestone walkway, the arrangement looks as if it is floating above the cabinets.

The center of the arrangement is made from a base of variegated pittosporum and lady's mantle. The last step is to add clusters of bright yellow and pale green mini gerberas.

lemon basket

This arrangement makes me think of a game of tennis on a summer afternoon. One glance and I'm longing for a glass of homemade lemonade or a slice of luscious lemon cake. I can't think of anything more perfect. The arrangement is simple to make, even if it doesn't look it. Start with a chicken-wire collar around a plastic bowl. Make it in the same way as the collar for the golden shower orchids (see page 44). Wire up the lemons by sticking a length of medium wire through the center of each and twisting the ends of the wire together, then wire a lower row of lemons to the collar, followed by an upper one. Fill the plastic bowl with crumpled chicken wire, add the water, and finally position the flowers and foliage.

This audacious arrangement of yellow and orange rose heads was designed to make a stunning impact on a console table in a formal hallway. It certainly adds a touch of the unexpected with its sizzling colors and rough wood container. I could also see a tray of roses like this one gracing the center of a large dining table, where its low lines would not impede dinner-table conversation. If you are handy, you can easily make a container like mine from rough wood planks and some thick rope. When not being used for roses, it would look equally appealing filled with rows of red and green apples or with walnuts and chestnuts.

Roses are expensive to buy, and I use a large quantity of them here—in fact over a hundred 'Pareo' and 'Golden Gates'—so this really is an arrangement for a special occasion. You will want the roses to last as long as possible, so you should give them a good long drink of water before you arrange them. Also, you should make sure the wooden tray is well lined with heavy plastic to prevent water from leaking out.

rows of roses

1

Carefully line a wooden tray with heavy plastic, making sure the plastic comes well up the sides of the tray.

2

Fill the tray with blocks of florist's foam that have been soaked in a bucket of water for several hours.

3

Remove any foliage and trim the stems of the roses at an angle. Arrange the first row of rose heads along the side of the tray.

4

Add more rose heads until one block of color is complete.

5

Continue adding roses, alternating the blocks of color until the tray is full.

foxtail lilies

The sunshine yellow of the wall is complemented by the yellow foxtail lilies, and the handrail by the cattails and millet grass. The base of green and yellow variegated euonymus gives the arrangement a lift, while the foxtail lilies, with their very solid, rather heavy stems, add a relaxed feel.

LEFT

One of the things I love about this mixture of flowers is their similarity of shape and form. They are all predominantly spiky but have different textures. The compact density of the millet grass reflects that of the cattails. The long stems of foxtail lilies are similar in shape, but have a looser habit. The air between each flower gives them a light and elegant feel.

This striking arrangement shows the beautiful harmonies that can be created using the full range of yellows, from pale, greenish-yellow to dark rusty orange. It was when I was decorating a friend's house for a party that I noticed this spot on the landing. It needed a large and fairly classical arrangement, so I filled a great black cast-iron urn with a mass of late-summer flowers. I would have preferred to arrange the flowers in water, but because the bowl of the urn was too small for a large enough water-holding container, I had to arrange them in wet florist's foam, which is not quite so satisfactory. Using quality flowers like these, you will want the arrangement to last as long as possible, so top up the water daily. If you pick off the lower flowers of the foxtail lilies as they fade, they can last two weeks or more.

For a late-summer arrangement, line a crate with plastic sheeting and plant it with yellow sunflowers. This is the perfect size to place in the middle of a buffet table for a summer party, to give the table some height.

If I had used a rose with a bigger head to decorate this hat, I would have used only three, but whatever the size, my rule of thumb is to always use clusters of flowers in odd numbers—threes, fives, sevens, and so on.

spirit of summer

The full, open heads of roses and the happy, smiling faces of sunflowers both capture the spirit of summer. The crate that in winter was filled with dried yellow roses (see page 42) is now planted with yellow sunflowers. The woven hat, looking almost like a basket of thin cane, was crying out for a trimming of summer grasses and roses. First I made a strip of braided grass, that I attached around the crown like a hatband. Then I picked a simple bunch of meadow grass from a hedgerow, folded the end of the bunch back on itself, and anchored it with a thick wire to the braided grass band. You could use sotol if meadow grass is not available. Finally, I wired five coffee-colored 'Safari' roses onto the grass band with some more stems of meadow grass.

Tulips are ideal cut flowers, because from the minute you buy them they keep on changing their form and character. You can watch them develop from tight buds into open blooms, and then fade—the process is fascinating. Whether you indulge in huge bunches of field-grown varieties or yearn for the simplicity of a single 'Black Parrot' tulip, there truly are tulips for every style and mood. Tulips are not renowned for their scent, but for their variety of different shapes. There are feathered Parrot tulips, pointed Lily-flowered tulips, and the traditional turban style. Since they are available most of the year, they are a boon for flower arrangers.

tulips

BELOW

The wonderful thing about
tulips is that they can be placed
casually in a simple glass vase
like this and left to do their
own thing.

RIGHT

What could be simpler than a
row of glass bottles, each
holding just one double tulip?
They make a great display on a
kitchen windowsill or on a
narrow tabletop.

I remember tulips well from my student days at the Royal Horticultural Society gardens at Wisley, in Surrey, so I have a special
fondness for them. We used to use them as a spring bedding plant—yellow 'Bellona' early single tulips with a soft haze of pale blue
forget-me-nots as an underplanting for the roses in the formal rose garden. Nowadays I find the long-stemmed French
varieties, single or double, and in a wonderful range of colors, very exciting. I also love miniature tulips, which can successfully be
grown in pots and brought indoors.

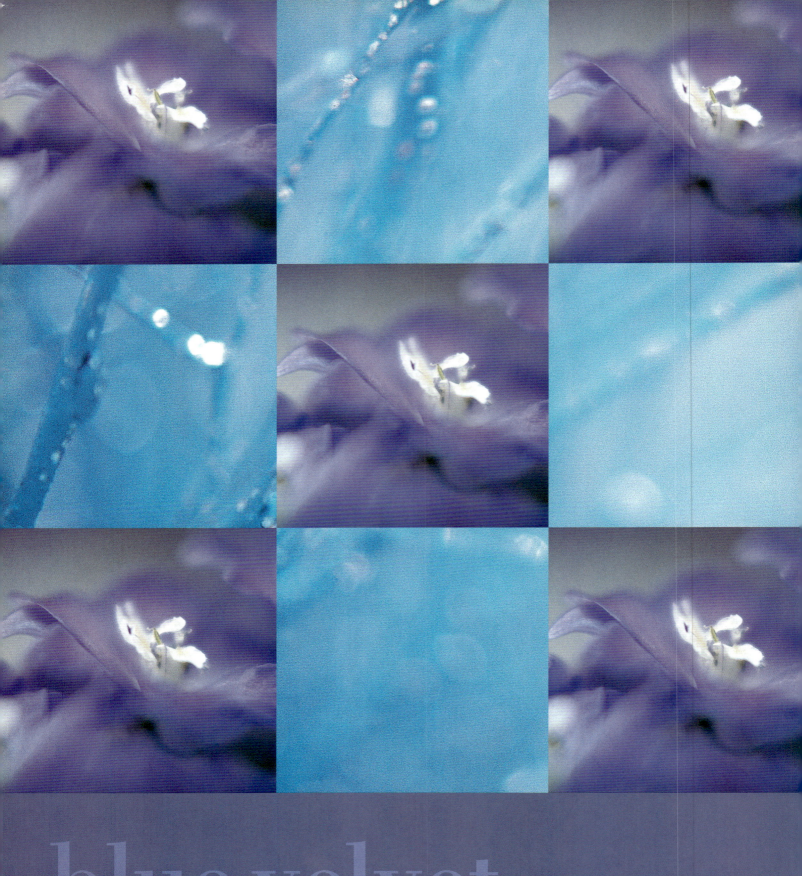

blue velvet

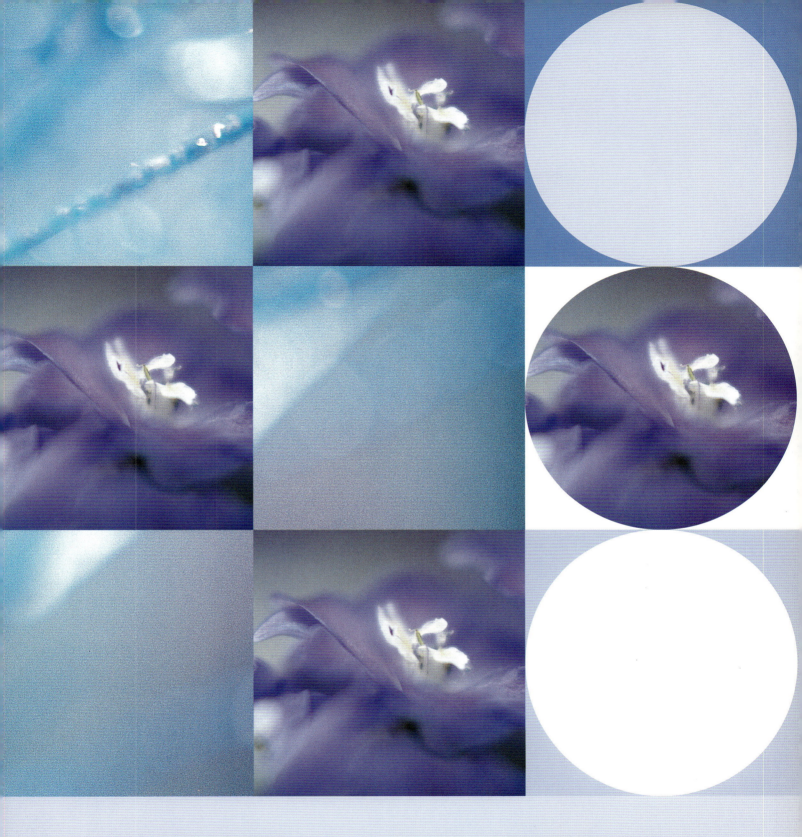

Blue reminds me of spring. I love it when the woods near my home are covered in hazy drifts of bluebells, like a dreamlike patchwork quilt. Blue also makes me think of the sea, from soft gray-blue under a winter sky to the clear green-blue of a sunlit sea. I have only to put together a bunch of sea holly with driftwood and pebbles to conjure up an image of a sun-bleached seaside garden. Blue is also for relaxation, mystery, and coolness. If I add blue flowers to a mixed arrangement, it lends it an air of subtlety and calm.

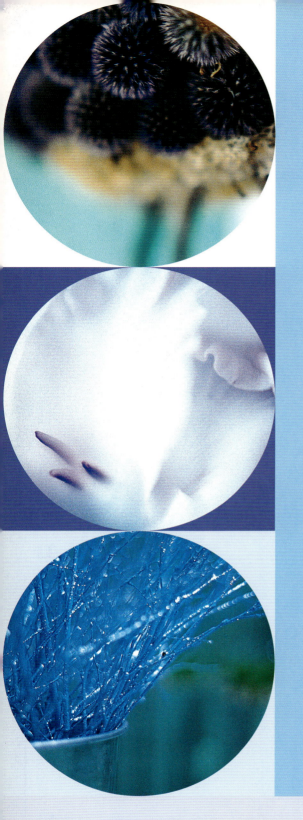

Nature looks so perfect dressed in blue. It never ceases to amaze me that glistening globe thistles can grow to such a wonderful shape, or that blues can come as delicate as this misty gladiolus flower. The blue-sprayed silver birch twigs look positively ethereal with their dusting of silver.

Blues come in many guises. Soft blues are traditional for a newborn baby boy, but dark blues send a more powerful message. Deep blue hyacinths and delphiniums resonate alongside purple lisianthus, but add white flowers, such as tulips or snapdragons for a crisp, nautical effect. I love blues in the garden, too, especially in combination with silver-gray foliage. Lavender, with its beautiful flower and foliage colors and its heavenly scent, has it all, while my favorite blue climbing plant is wisteria.

Grape hyacinths are one of my favorite spring bulbs. They look stunning massed together, in the garden or in a vase. This vase is perfect for them. Its sexy curves echo the curves of the tiny, individual, bell-like flowers.

For this classic look, put a mass of delphiniums together. Place the tallest stems—all cut to the same length—first, then support them with a few shorter ones at the front.

In general, garden-grown delphiniums shed their petals indoors sooner than the cultivated ones, but I find that the dark blue *D.* (Belladonna Group) 'Blue Bees,' the cream *D.* (Belladonna Group) 'Casa Blanca,' and the white Pacific Giant hybrids shown here all last well as cut flowers.

delphiniums

Traditionally a cottage-garden plant, delphiniums are flowers I love to grow in an herbaceous bed. They add so much drama. They are the only flowers I know that have such strongly defined spires in the blue color range. They can grow very tall and so need staking. Sometimes I use these very long stems to add stateliness to an arrangement, but the smaller-flowered cultivated varieties are wonderful, too. Some of the colors have a luster to them that gives them an almost crystalline translucency. Putting all the shades together like this makes them look almost unreal. They certainly don't need any more adornment.

The violets stand in simple terracotta pots. The saucers have been painted silver, and the pots a lilac color. This shade of lilac works well with the silver and gives the whole arrangement an easy-to-live-with, modern feel. I have arranged the pots in three rows of three, like a living sculpture.

The violet, with its strong, vibrant jewellike depth of color, its contrasting dark green veined leaves, and its heady scent, is a wonderfully old-fashioned flower. It is not the easiest flower to use in arrangements, as it has a short stem and wilts very quickly. I am not sure if that is the origin of the term "shrinking violet." If you do decide to use violets, be sure to re-cut their stems and place in water immediately. If you can't find cut violets, you can achieve the same look by using purple African violet plants. These would have the advantage of lasting a lot longer. This composition would also work well with single blue hyacinth bulbs or with acid-green baby's tears.

violets

A glass liner inside each pot holds the water and three bunches of violets edged with their leaves.

It's best to make the tree when the branches have no leaves on them. At that stage they are pliable, but not so soft that they cannot take any weight. Kept out of strong sunlight, the thistles will hold their natural blue color for many years. To stop the tree from getting dusty, periodically wave a hairdryer, on a cold setting, over it. The tree smells wonderful sprinkled with lavender oil.

For a cloud tree, you need stems of Harry Lauder's walking stick or Hangkow willow in a pot filled with quick-setting plaster. As the plaster dries, it may crack the pot, so use a plastic one that will fit into an outer pot. Attach clumps of chicken wire to the stems, fill the chicken wire with moss, then wire up the individual thistle heads and anchor them to the moss, starting with the lowest row of each cloud. To disguise the mechanics, glue gray lichen to the underside of each cloud. Make an odd number of clouds, arranging them with the largest at the bottom of the tree and the smallest at the top.

This arrangement of Hankow willow or Harry Lauder's walking stick with globe thistles looks just like soft clouds caught up in the branches of a tree. It was inspired by the modern, asymmetrical look of the fireplace. It's more common to use an evenly spaced pair of containers on a mantelpiece, but because of the way the wall behind was painted, I felt the left-hand side of the scheme needed emphasizing to adjust the balance. I also thought that the strictness of the painted wall and fireplace would look better with the soft lines of a cloud tree than if I had used a more formal topiary tree.

blue cloud tree

The shape of this tree reminds
me of the Cedar of Lebanon,
which grows in many old,
established gardens.

Christmas is a time when people like to decorate their front doors with a wreath to welcome their guests. Here, I have taken the traditional Christmas wreath but have given it a new slant by using shades of blue instead of the usual green, red, and gold. The wreath is not as difficult as it looks. I started with a circle of wire covered with moss, then attached a base of blue spruce, arranged so that its tips all followed the line of the circle. Next, I added crisscrossed clusters of lavender, all cut to the same length and tied with raffia. Last to go in were the groups of white gourds and bunches of eucalyptus pods. A wreath like this should last for about four weeks.

I love using eucalyptus pods, not only because of their fascinating shape but also because of their color—a lovely cool blue-green. They are, in fact, flowers whose petals fuse together as they mature. When the top of the pod falls off, the stamens appear. These have that familiar eucalyptus aroma.

gourd wreath

This conservatory seemed to me to be the perfect location for a tower of glass cones in a metal frame planted with blue hyacinths. The arrangement works well with the surrounding hard materials—the alloy frame and the corrugated metal walls of the conservatory—while the blue of the hyacinths complements the glass walls. The fact that the hyacinths are growing softens the whole effect. I couldn't wait to get the finished tower into position and love the reflection of it all in the mirror. An alternative to planting the hyacinths in a tower like this would be simply to plant them in a deep glass dish. That would look stunningly cosmopolitan sitting on a glass coffee or dining table.

towering hyacinths

1

Supporting the cone in a deep container, line it with gray lichen. Place some drainage material such as gravel or clay granules in the bottom.

2

Select an odd number of forced hyacinth bulbs. They should all be at the same stage of development.

3

Plant the hyacinths, adding plenty of potting mix around their roots, then water well and top off with more gray lichen.

sea holly & roses

FAR LEFT AND LEFT
The fleshy round heads of the roses and sea holly contrast sharply with the sea holly's jagged, silvery bracts and with the fine stems of the eucalyptus. The color contrasts double the effect of the contrasts of shape.

I love having a neutral background to which I can add an element of surprise in the form of unexpected color. In this setting, I started with a subtle palette of tones—cream, white, and beige. For contrast, I have chosen a translucent blue vase. Placed on a glass table in a window, the vase is backlit, revealing the lovely outline of the stems of the flowers and foliage. The base of this arrangement is flowering eucalyptus and *Brachyglottis* 'Sunshine.' Then I added the lush stems of sea holly, with its sea-anemone-type flower in silver-blue. Next I wove in some stems of purple lisianthus, with its cup-shaped flowers, and finally I added orange 'Pareo' roses. The zingy combination of orange with purple is great, adding a dose of vitality to the arrangement.

The driftwood is a subtle silver-gray that complements beautifully the blue of the anemones. It also provides a color and shape link with the chrome legs of the table. The driftwood and the pebbles are magnified by the water, which adds another dimension to this unusual arrangement.

This design was created for a fiftieth birthday party for someone who is passionate about fishing. So what could be better, I thought, than to include fish in the table decoration? With this in mind, I placed a goldfish in its bowl in a circular dish filled with wet florist's foam and studded the foam with rings of blue anemones, starting at the outer edge, and finishing as close as I could to the goldfish bowl. The anemones make the water look blue and contrast beautifully with the color of the fish. For extra interest, I put some pebbles in the bottom of the bowl and included two pieces of driftwood to introduce the idea of the water's link with the land.

anemones & driftwood

lined-up blues

To underscore the geometry of this arrangement, I spent some time cutting all the stems of lavender to the same length. This gives the arrangement a flat, tabletop effect that works well with the straight-sided metal pots.

The row of vases reflects the strict design of the balcony, while the bachelor's buttons give a relaxed, rural feel. They almost look as if they are growing. Seeing their stems through the frosted glass reminds me of hazy summer skies.

Depending on what you put in them, rows of matching pots or vases can suit modern or traditional locations. Lavender is usually associated with traditional country interiors. A mass of it stuffed into an old terracotta pot looks as if it has just been picked from the yard. That same concept, but approached in a contemporary way, can work in a modern setting, too. For a classic interior that has been modernized, my choice was three square matching galvanized metal pots placed in a row and crammed with cut lavender. These pots would also look superb filled with baby's tears plants. These come in acid green, lime green, variegated gold, and plain green varieties to suit any color scheme.

To complement my old French wrought-iron balcony, I opted for the simplicity of a row of frosted glass vases filled with blue bachelor's buttons, arranged very loosely and informally. I like the mix of the modern, crisp, frosted glass with the old, characterful balcony. This arrangement would also be successful using Iceland poppies. With their loose habit and long stems, they are similar to the bachelor's buttons.

A galvanized trash can and coordinating colors give a contemporary twist to a traditional Christmas tree. My preference is for white lights on any Christmas tree, but especially on this one, where white complements the silver of the trash can and the blue of the spray-painted branches. Stabilize the trash can by filling it with sand, and, if young children will be around, you might consider wiring the lower branches of the tree to the can handles as an extra safety precaution. Choose a tree with non-dropping needles, and use a mask and follow the manufacturer's instructions when you are applying the spray paint. When you arrange the lights in the tree, loop them along the length of the branches rather than round and round the tree. This distributes them more evenly and looks more natural. Check if the lights are well positioned by half-closing your eyes. The lights will seem to sparkle more, making it easier to judge the effect.

Christmas tree

1

Remove the bulbs from the Christmas tree lights, and spray the cord silver. Separate the branches of the tree using the flat of your hand.

2

Spray the branches with matte, pale blue paint, spraying up and down for even coverage.

3

Replace the bulbs and arrange the lights on the tree along the length of the branches.

4

Wire the blue ornaments onto the branches, taking care that they are evenly spaced.

These purplish-mauve gladioli are an astonishingly beautiful color. They really leap out at you. In this composition, the glass shapes edging the mirror reflect the shape of the individual gladiolius flowers.

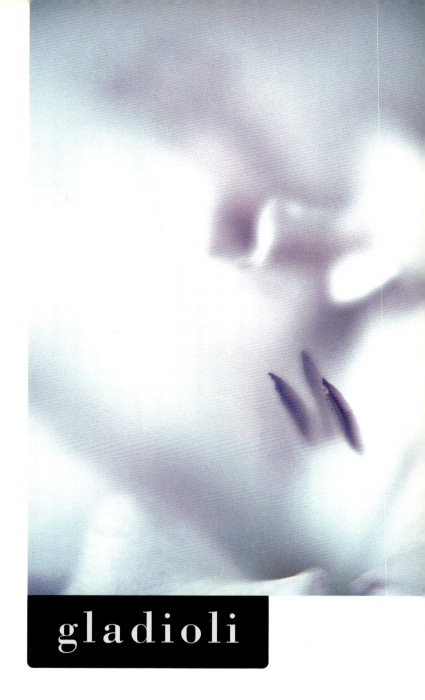

gladioli

Thanks to the minimalist movement in interior design, gladioli are staging a comeback. With their tall stems and strong, bold flowers in colors ranging from white, blue, yellow, red, burgundy and pink to an amazing green—'Green Woodpecker'—they are the flowers to watch for. They are also very versatile, looking just as good in an industrial-looking vase of metal rods lined with blown glass, or cut down and placed in small pots, so that the emphasis is on the beauty of their individual flowers. They also last an extremely long time. With long stems, you can take off the lower flowers as they fade. This enourages the buds to open.

Here I underline the architectural quality of the gladioli by using them in a concrete block installation on the floor. I have set a square metal vase in one cavity of the block, filling it with a mass of red gladioli. In the other, I have placed a glass of water with a pair of rolled-up dark green *Farfugium japonicum* leaves.

RIGHT, INSET
Laid along a shallow dish, single gladiolus flowers can make a very quick and simple table centerpiece. As an alternative, they would look great floating in water in a glass bowl.

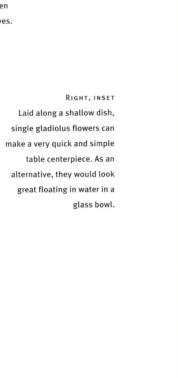

strawberry fields

As bright, strong colors take over in popularity from pastel shades, red has to be one of my favorites. It is linked with festivity and romance. Different tones of red can be found in many exciting flowers, in all the seasons, and across the full spectrum. You only have to think of dark red roses, magenta monarda, scarlet dahlias, or pale pink peonies. I often like to put shades of red together or, alternatively, to add another strong color such as purple, which makes for a very special and intense combination.

LEFT, FROM TOP

A pale pink gerbera, its center fringed with tiny darker petals, a medium-pink flowering prunus, and a cluster of fringed red and white Parrot tulips surrounded by suede-effect *Magnolia grandiflora* leaves show something of the range of red tones that Nature can produce.

Red is a color I use throughout the year. It is festive at Christmas and is the obvious choice for Valentine's Day. At the height of summer, I incorporate in my arrangements the lush soft fruits that are in season, while in the fall, reddish foliage is a must. Reds merge into purples with *Rosa glauca* (syn. *R. rubrifolia*), with the plum-red foliage of the smoke tree, and with the burgundy berries of hypericum. Reds become almost black with the flowers of chocolate cosmos which actually smell of chocolate.

I love the gradation of color in this pink calla lily, from the almost burgundy tips of its petals to its pale pink-veined center. Calla lilies come in other bright colors—burnt orange and yellow, for example—but the classic color is white.

This modern, blue wire mesh container gives the normally traditional peony a completely different, modern flavor. Here I have placed an odd number of medium-pink peonies—some of them double-flowered—around the rim of the container, and have filled in with dark red scented blooms.

Peonies are great as cut flowers and look equally appropriate in a contemporary or traditional arrangement. They are available in many varieties and a wonderful range of colors; some are even scented, which is a bonus. Most have the characteristic "over the top" size of bloom—I have seen some with heads as large as 10 in./25cm. across. Varieties that I love to grow for cutting include some cultivars of *Paeonia lactiflora*—the clear, pale pink 'Sarah Bernhardt,' the dark red 'Karl Rosenfield,' and the white, slightly blushed with pink 'Duchesse de Nemours.' Peonies can be dried rather easily, but require drying quickly so they will not drop their petals. Just hang them upside down in a very warm place for a couple of weeks. Once dried, they look teriffic as an edging for a basket of potpourri.

peonies

LEFT
This Dutch still-life-style
arrangement of peonies would
suit a country interior. I
especially love the trailing
scented jasmine. For evening,
the arrangement could be
enhanced with drifts of red
plums, cherries, and
strawberries around the base,
and red glass votive candles.

ABOVE
Dried peonies also look great.
Fill a terracotta pot with florist's
foam and top it with moss, then
place the peonies as you would
fresh ones, but closer together.
Because they shrink when
dried, you will need almost
twice as many blooms as for
the summer arrangement.

Following the principle of always using odd numbers, I have hung three clear glass test tubes from a stair rail and have put a stem of ornamental cabbage in each. What I love about using test tubes is the way they highlight the bold color of whatever they contain—in this case, the cut stems of the cabbages.

In the future, I am sure we shall be using more industrial-looking containers as flower holders. They really seem to capture the pared-down, industrial spirit of our age, but the effect is softened by the wonderful blooms they contain. These two arrangements show how much can be achieved simply by lining up a number of beautiful, individual specimens in a row. First I used ornamental cabbages, which are among my favorite plants. I like white ones best of all, but they also come in green, as well as in the pink I have used here. Whenever I plan a kitchen garden, I always add a few of these plants for fun. They look terrific in containers, too. In the other arrangement I have used four elegant, sinuous pink calla lilies. Like the cabbages, they look stunning all in a row.

BELOW
The clean lines of this metal-framed test-tube holder and the clarity of its glass tubes make a marvelous container for single-stem specimens such as these wonderful pink calla lilies. Arranged in this way, the individual beauty of each flower becomes part of a strong whole.

sinuous shapes

Red is such a strong color that often it needs nothing more than the green of its foliage to set it off. These arrangements demonstrate that point to perfection. The terracotta pot would make a wonderful centerpiece for an autumn dinner party, or would look stunning placed on a side table under a lamp to bring out the richness of its colors. The basket of red cyclamen makes a truly eye-catching gift and would provide more long-lasting pleasure than a bouquet of flowers. These miniature red cyclamen are slightly scented and, as long as you pick off any dead flowers, will last for many weeks. As a complete contrast, the minimalist arrangement of burgundy Persian ranunculus would be ideal for a crisp, modern table setting. Ranunculus flowers are so perfect, you might almost think they were made from tissue paper.

LEFT
This arrangement consists of berried ivy, cotoneaster berries, hypericum, pokeweed, ornamental crab apple, burgundy snapdragons, red nerines, and clusters of 'Vicky Brown' roses. I have also used a red spray rose—'Tamango'—and spiky stems of *Pavonia* x *gledhillii* pods to give the arrangement some strength.

BELOW
Here I garlanded a basket with long, twining stems of honeysuckle to add interesting texture and to make the basket look less artificial. Make sure you line the basket well with double-thickness plastic to prevent water from leaking out.

fire and ice

The black-lacquered tray of
champagne glasses
filled with raffia-tied Persian
ranunculus shows that it is not
flowers alone that make a
successful arrangement.

hand-tied roses

No matter what the occasion—a special celebration, a thank-you, or simply a romantic gesture—a bunch of roses always makes a welcome present. There are so many beautiful varieties around now, but my favorites are 'Nicole'—raspberry with a whitish undercolor; 'Vicky Brown'—reddish-brown, with an undercolor like tan suede; and the 'Black Magic' shown here—a stunning velvety dark red. It's very easy to make a hand-tied bouquet like this one. If you first make the basic shape with the foliage, the rest will fall into place. Here I have used five pieces of berried ivy, with their lower leaves removed. Then I added twelve long-stemmed roses—lower leaves and thorns removed and stems cut at an angle—placing them slightly higher than the foliage in the center, and slightly deeper around the edges to produce a gentle mound. If roses are too traditional for your taste, any round-headed flowers would do. Anemones or gerberas would give a more contemporary look.

1

Holding the ivy in one hand, arrange it into a bouquet.

2

Thread the roses through, spacing them equally throughout and trying to maintain a slightly rounded shape to the bouquet.

3

Using a piece of raffia, tie the bouquet together fairly high up the stems, then trim the stems all to the same length.

4

Fold several layers of white tissue paper so they form two points.

5

Wrap the tissue paper around the bouquet, then repeat with a second layer of paper.

6

Wrap in clear cellophane, then tie with a bow made of strands of raffia. Finish by trimming the ends of the raffia bow.

With a lovely summer's evening and a willow-tree backdrop that was the very willow of Kenneth Grahame's *The Wind in the Willows*, a special table setting was called for. The burgundy velvet tablecloth is smothered with a profusion of rich tones—purple sage, mint, hyssop, thyme, flat-leaved parsley, and spikes of purple heuchera, all brimming out of old terracotta pots. More pots are filled with heads of 'Only Love' roses, with the spray red rose 'Domingo,' with chocolate cosmos and stems of fruiting blackberry.

wind in the willows

Drifts of fruit laid on dark green
leaves to enhance their color,
together with clusters of red
glass votive candles,
complement the herbs and
flowers. At each place setting is
a potted herb, its plant label
serving as a placecard. Sprigs of
love-lies-bleeeding emphasize
the gathers of the tablecloth.

These two arrangements, with their soft, dusky pinks, lilacs, and toned-down reds are the epitome of summer and romance. The mixed arrangement in a smart, trumpet-shaped frosted vase is my idea of "shabby chic"—flowers with a slightly shabby coloration in a chic location. Even though the arrangement is made from fresh flowers, it reminds me of old, gently faded botanical prints. The feeling of romance continues with the arrangement of belladonna lilies (also called amaryllis) —clear pastel pink flowers with the most unbelievable soft, soapy fragrance. They have a pure, old-fashioned quality to them that I find completely irresistible.

summer romance

A cluster of belladonna lilies accompanied by the mauve-purple foliage of *Rosa glauca* syn. R. *rubrifolia* stands in a simple but stunning glass vase.

A subdued color scheme is created by using flag irises in a base of eucalyptus and *Rosa glauca* syn. R. *rubrifolia* foliage. There are also clusters of dark purple and lilac-colored stocks, sprays of 'Sterling Silver' roses, and bursts of washed-out plum-colored 'Iced Tea' roses.

I do like putting flowers, fruits, and other ingredients behind glass or Lucite. It adds another dimension, magnifying and highlighting their color. Here I filled a glass vase with water, then submerged in it whole stems of ornamental red peppers. You can see how the stems are enlarged and their color enhanced.

red hot peppers

A single stem of peppers in a beer can hanging on a wall looks like a three-dimensional work of art—completely unarranged, yet very striking.

Rising above a glass vase filled with red ornamental peppers, two stems of red lobster claws stand tall above a flat collar of *Farfugium japonicum* leaves. The red of this striking arrangement stands out in its monochrome setting, bringing an exotic touch to a very urban environment.

Bright, shiny ornamental peppers have a raw sexiness about them. Their vivid colors look almost painted on, and they are so striking you dare not mix them with anything else. Containers need to be very simple, too, so they are not fighting for attention. The peppers come in different shapes—the red pointed variety used here, which is also available in yellow, orange, and an apricot color, and another variety with small round fruits in orange, yellow, and red.

This arrangement of pastel shades of sweet peas and lady's mantle in a container of cut broom is a breath of summer. If you were using it as a centerpiece for a dinner party, the leftover pieces of broom could be used to tie up the napkins. Once the broom has dried out, you could use the basket for a fall arrangement. When buying sweet peas, try to find long-life-treated varieties, as these last considerably longer.

Starting with a plastic bowl, make a chicken-wire collar, as on page 44. Place the wire collar over a piece of moss that is as deep as the bowl and will wrap around it, then fold the wire around the moss. Attach this moss collar firmly around the bowl with a crisscrossed wire. Assemble lengths of broom and use thick wire to hold the ends together in bunches. Wrap the broom bunches around the moss collar and anchor with more thick wire. Repeat until the moss is completely covered, using thin wire at intervals to pull the broom in tight against the moss.

Fill the container with crumpled chicken wire, then half-fill with water. Make sure that no moss is hanging over the edges into the container, as this will siphon water off and can cause staining if you place the arrangement on an unprotected surface. You then need to create the foundation of the arrangement. In this case I have used large clusters of lady's mantle. Finish with small bunches of three stems of sweet peas in two or three shades. Fill around the edges first to create a cascading effect, then add more bunches from the top of the arrangement.

a basket of sweet peas

1 Fold chicken wire around a length of moss to make a moss collar and anchor around the bowl.

2 Wrap lengths of broom around the moss collar, wiring them in to give the effect of a basket of broom.

3

Place large clusters of lady's mantle into the container to form a solid sturdy base.

4

Create a lush effect, adding bunches of sweet peas, first around the edges, then from above.

It always amazes me that a red
as strong as this can be natural.
How I would love to have this
arrangement sitting on my desk.
It shows how the individual
beauty of a single bloom can be
as effective as a whole bunch. In
this case, less truly is more.

 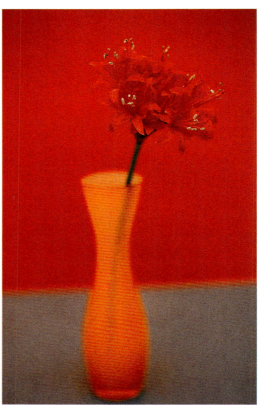

Here, one arrangement is purely classical, the other starkly modern—but what unites the two is the zingy orange and the curvaceous lines of the two vases. The rusty urn's classic shape makes it work really well with the objects around it—the old figurines, the cornucopias, and the lions and griffons. But I think it's the urn's faded grandeur that gives the arrangement its edge. In the case of the single stem of red nerine, part of the arrangement's power comes from the terrific little vase. Its bold color and simple shape make it a thing of beauty in its own right. Together with the red nerine, it is unbeatable.

sizzling oranges

FAR LEFT AND ABOVE
Tall spikes of *Rosa glauca* syn.
R. rubrifolia and of smoke tree
give this warm-toned
arrangement its outline. Depth
is added with the interwoven
clusters of 'Leonardis' roses,
while the orange 'Pareo' roses
give the arrangement more
punch. Whitebeam berries add a
slight autumnal flavor.

This unusual container is plastic, covered with sprigs of box wired in small bunches onto a chicken-wire collar (see page 104). The base is of *Skimmia japonica* 'Rubella,' followed by scarlet plume, 'James Storey' orchids, and clusters of blood-red 'Black Magic' roses.

red exuberance

You can't beat a whole mass of Parrot tulips. This variety—'Estella Rijnveld'—looks really great edged in the very characteristic glossy dark green leaves of *Magnolia grandiflora*, with their brown suede undercolor.

The interplay of foliage and flowers makes these two arrangements special. In one, an eruption of frothy, fringed bicolor tulips is brought under control by a corset of strict *Magnolia grandiflora* leaves, tightly tied with raffia. In the other, the exuberance of the arching stems of scarlet plume and of the 'James Storey' orchids is given free rein. Only the sturdy container grounds the composition. Either arrangement would suit a modern interior, though the juxtaposition of the more traditional one with the bare loft is slightly unexpected, though none the worse for that.

gerberas

When I go to buy flowers at the market, gerberas are always on my shopping list. I love their strong, open-faced simplicity. There is nothing coy or affected about them. They simply are what they are. Despite their unaffected appearance, they are very versatile for flower arranging, looking great either as single blooms—in colored plastic glasses, they almost look plastic themselves—in single-color or multicolor masses, or as the "star performers" of a mixed arrangement, punctuating it with bold, round splashes of color. I usually use gerberas as cut flowers, but what fun a mass of mixed plants proves to be planted in an old wooden trug.

This is flower power at its best. Nothing more than a simple bunch of pure white gerberas in a curvy, frosted glass vase, or heads of deep red 'Chateau' gerberas floating in a bowl of silver-lacquered bamboo leaves. Seen close up, the two-tone centers sparkle like the iris of an eye.

Part of the gerbera's versatility lies in its wide range of colors—from white through pale pink, red, and burgundy to medium brown, orange, and yellow, and many variations in between. But even the single-color flowers have touches of contrast, either in the stamens in the center of the flower or in the tiny petals that sometimes surround the center. Occasionally a stem will be damaged and the head will droop. If this happens, either cut the stem off and use the flower head on its own—they look wonderful floating in water—or attach a piece of florist's wire to the back of each flower and twist the end around the stem to hold it in place.

a whiter shade of pale

For years it has been argued that white is not a color; but for me as well as for that great fashion guru Coco Chanel, white is my favorite. It is bright and eye-catching, yet also soothing, and it looks fabulous used by itself, but equally good with any other color. It certainly doesn't need to be boring, as no two whites are the same. In fact, in the world of flowers at least, there is no such thing as a pure white. You will find it tinged with yellow, green, pink, or blue.

LEFT, FROM TOP
These three flowers are all
white, but are totally different
shades. Pink-tinged tuberose
has a wonderful, romantic
perfume, clouds of prunus
blossom are a harbinger of
spring, while the tiny, tubular
white flowers of bells of Ireland
hide coyly away in their shell-
like calyx.

I don't think you can go wrong with white flowers. They bring purity to any garden design or flower arrangement; and although all-white gardens have long been popular, the minimalist movement has made them especially so in recent years. For me, white tulips are the epitome of minimalist white flowers. I would like nothing more than a mass of them in the center of my dining table—all year round if that were possible, though I do prefer to use flowers in their correct season.

When you look at
this jasmine, with its
beautiful pink-tinged
petals, you can almost
smell its wonderful, heady
fragrance. I always associate
this flower with late spring, as
that is when it is at its best.

For support, the orchids are tied to stakes with natural raffia. To maintain this arrangement for as long as possible, keep it out of direct sunlight. Since the bowl has no drainage, do not overwater; otherwise, the young roots will rot.

driftwood & orchids

Pieces of driftwood, together
with the pebbles and the
yellow-beige centers of the
orchids, complement the earth
colors of the abstract painting
in the background.

Orchids, with their beautifully sculpted flowers, bring a touch of exoticism to any room. They come in colors ranging from hot pink to green to the recently introduced chocolate brown. But to my mind, nothing beats white ones. Here I have planted three white phalenopsis orchids in a deep glass bowl. Unless I am using a plant that has an interesting root system, I always like to line glass bowls with some material such as moss, fruit, or bark chips, which are then seen through the glass. In this case, I used some beautiful sea-washed gray pebbles along with gray lichen. The final touch was the pieces of weathered driftwood.

agapanthus & swiss cheese

The crisp white of the flowers and the glossy, green leaves work well with the wooden paneling and the old chest of drawers. The arrangement has a strong, crisp, tropical feel to it.

These two arrangements are variations on a theme, and show that, with care, the same ingredients can work in either a small-scale or a large-scale arrangement. I love white agapanthus, but it is a very busy-looking flower, so it needs to be balanced by something with strong, graphic lines. The dark green glossy leaves of the swiss cheese plant, also called Mexican breadfruit, fit the bill perfectly. For the vase standing on the small chest of drawers, I have used a small-flowering form of agapanthus—*A.* 'Bressingham White'—and small swiss cheese plant leaves, while for the striking floor arrangement a bolder statement was needed, so I used a larger-flowering agapanthus—*A. praecox* subsp. *maximus* 'Albus'—and bigger swiss cheese leaves.

This wooden floor needed a
very simple but large-scale
statement. The bold leaves of
the swiss cheese plant provide
the perfect background for a
mass of long white agapanthus
stems in a plain, upright vase.

Here I lined the glass vase with the bold, round leaves of *Farfugium japonicum*, then cut all the stems of the papyrus to the same length to form a radiating dome.

Who needs flowers when we have this wonderful grass? With its strong graphic identity and bright green color, papyrus is ideally suited to the clean, crisp lines of today's interiors. Here I have used it in two very formal arrangements, but a couple of stems placed in a narrow Lucite vase also look terrific—very minimalist. As an added bonus, papyrus also works well when it is dried, so you can use it fresh in one arrangement, then dried in another. Once dry, it turns a lovely soft sage green that looks best in a ceramic container.

The inspiration for this two-tiered arrangement of papyrus grass was the vase. I trimmed the papyrus to a very exact shape, then broke up the formal lines with some spikes of horsetail. The finished result has a rather oriental feel to it.

papyrus grass

Constance Spry brought the art of flower arranging into the English public eye after the gloomy war years. This shape of vase is very much associated with her style, so I wanted to use it for an arrangement in tribute to her. I filled it with a mixture of assorted greenery to show that a perfect display does not necessarily need to include any flowers. The kinds of foliage shown here often appear in my garden designs. Instead of having to prune them at specific times, you can simply cut them when they are needed for flower arrangements. They include *Viburnum tinus*, *Hedera canariensis* 'Gloire de Marengo,' two types of eucalyptus, Mexican orange, *Rosa glauca* syn. *R. rubrifolia*, *Euonymus japonicus* 'Aureus,' and *Brachyglottis* 'Sunshine.'

The varied textures of the different kinds of foliage evoke an old-fashioned sense of style that is best suited to a classic interior. With a neutral-colored container such as this one, you could, if you wanted, add flowers of any color. I would choose shades of red. Reds and greens always make a successful pairing.

formal foliage

flower-garlanded mirror

Grinling Gibbons (1648-1721) was the master of woodcarving, often using his exceptional skills to make frames for paintings or mirrors. He was my inspiration for this idea for a classic Victorian bedroom, designed to look as if it is made of carved wood. In order to achieve this effect, I limited myself to using graphic-shaped flowers, and even added a few roses made out of wood shavings. The garland also brings out the colors of the small, wooden objects on the mantelpiece. When you choose the frame for your mirror, bear in mind that by the time you have added the dried flowers, the whole thing will be larger than when you started. Although it may look difficult to make the garland, it is relatively easy; and once it is finished, it will last for many years.

1

Secure wide lengths of chicken
wire to a wooden mirror frame
with a staple gun.

2

Lay strips of dried moss on top,
then fold in the long edges of
the wire to hold the moss in
place around the frame.

3

Form the wheat into clusters,
their stems trimmed to one
length, then wire five evenly
spaced groups of crisscrossed
clusters to the moss.

4

Wire up bunches of single and double feverfew and *Rhodanthe chlorocephalem* syn. *Helipterum roseum*, and add them next, evenly spaced.

5

Fill in with clusters of dried poppy heads, white peonies, the wood-shaving roses, and the white roses.

With their long, slender stems and the edges of their flowers tinged with green, these Amazon lilies look stunning with a necklace of *Hedera canariensis* 'Gloire de Marengo.' The Amazon lilies are excellent as cut flowers. As the flowers fade, remove them, and the buds will continue to bloom.

solo whites

When you are arranging white flowers, you must take special care that the container you use complements the flowers and does not overwhelm them. This square-shaped, metallic vase, narrow at the base and wider at the top, was perfect for the natural, loose look I wanted to achieve with my beautiful bunch of white lilac and eucalyptus. The height of the vase was an added bonus, as it meant that I didn't have to cut the lilac down too much. Sadly, lilac does not last very well in an arrangement, but you can improve its chances if you cut the stems at an angle, so creating the largest possible surface area to take up water. The square frosted vase holding the wonderful scented Amazon lilies has a heavy base and is tall, which means that it, too, lends itself to a tall arrangement.

summer celebration

It's always rewarding to be asked to make an arrangement for a special occasion, like this one for a golden wedding anniversary. Starting with a simple glass dish with a ring of wet florist's foam on top, use double-sided tape to anchor three glass votive candles in the base, then fill the dish three-quarters full of water and set four church candles in the foam ring. Fill the ring with the foliage, then add the scented white flowers—long spikes of white stocks, groups of three stems of white sweet peas, and finally, clusters of three or five large-headed white 'Tineke' and 'Margaret Merril' roses. I love the way the light from the votive candles ripples out across the table.

LEFT AND BELOW
The foliage base works
perfectly well on its own. To
make it, you need variegated
pittosporum, *Brachyglottis*
'Sunshine,' cotton lavender,
variegated dracena, and some
gaultheria leaves.

LEFT
Adding white flowers to the
arrangement gives it a more
classic, romantic
dimension—perfect for a
wedding. If you added red
flowers instead, it would be
great for a Valentine's Day party
or a ruby wedding anniversary,
while blue and yellow flowers
would look good at a summer
gathering. With lovely weather,
you don't need any other excuse
for a party.

LEFT, ABOVE
Large geometric shapes like this lichen tree suit an uncluttered contemporary interior.

LEFT
You could try making a small lichen tree in a galvanized metal pot if the larger one is too daunting.

LEFT

The decoration of this apartment is a play on circles, squares, and rectangles. A circular white bowl stands on a wooden chest; a rectangular white frame contains a circular mirror. This, plus the plain white walls, sets the tone for an unusual installation.

RIGHT

Wired-on glass tubes hold white anthurium flowers. As the flowers fade, they can be replaced, making an ever-changing feature.

indoor trees

A modern location sometimes demands you be as much an engineering wizard as an arranger of flowers. For my palm-leaf tree, I made the main stem from a piece of plastic pipe pushed through three blocks of florist's foam. Next I wrapped the pipe in steel cable held on with glue, then covered the foam blocks with palm leaves. The tree is held in place with quick-setting cement in a cube-shaped galvanized container topped with gray lichen. The lichen trees are made from lichen-covered foam. Once again, for the tall tree, the stem is wrapped in steel cable and the planter topped off with lichen. These trees are very good for situations with low levels of light or with only artificial light, where no other tree-sized plant would survive.

This lovely glass tube snake, consisting of a metal frame supporting clear glass tubes, can be manipulated into different shapes. To set it off, I have chosen single stems of white nerines (also called Guernsey lilies) together with a beautiful variegated papyrus, folded and tied into loops using raffia. I have also included a few bunches of plain green papyrus, cut to the same length and again tied with raffia, and have tucked single galax leaves around the stems of some of the nerines so the leaves show through the glass. The container is very versatile. I love it as a centerpiece with narcissi on page 46, and think it would also look great with blue anemones and sprigs of eucalyptus. It would even lend itself to a Christmas arrangement with red roses and holly.

white nerine snake

In order to emphasize the horizontals in this arrangement, I have taken care to fill the glass tubes with water only up to or just above the line of the metal holder. This gives a more interesting look to the stems and leaves, magnifying those that are below the water line. Clear glass marbles at the bottom of each tube would also look good, especially if you were using flowers such as violets or primulas that have very short stems.

Subtlety and harmony are often the best options for a mixed arrangement, and this one is nothing if not subtle. The foliage is *Magnolia grandiflora*, an evergreen that is often seen as a climber up the walls of old country houses, though it can also be grown as a topiary tree in a small garden. Its suede underside has a lovely texture, and it is this, plus its color, that works so well with the chestnuts and walnuts lining the glass bowl. The addition of just one very choice type of flower could not be bettered. Originally natives of Mexico, tuberoses, with their heady fragrance, are among my favorite flowers. Their spiky, architectural flowerheads echo the shape of the magnolia leaves. The combined weight of the tuberoses, with their heavy heads, the foliage, and the water is quite substantial, so you must make sure you use florist's tape to stick the plastic bowl carefully in place inside the glass container; otherwise, you risk having everything topple over.

tuberoses & nuts

1

Stand a rigid plastic bowl in the center of a glass dish, fix the bowl in place using florist's tape, then add water.

2

Put some crumpled chicken wire in the plastic bowl, then line the space between the bowl and the glass with alternating panels of walnuts and chestnuts.

3

Fill in with a base of *Magnolia grandiflora* leaves.

4

Finally, add single stems of tuberose, evenly spaced throughout the foliage.

At the height of summer, what could be more delightful than a hat decorated with blowsy, scented old garden roses? This design needs the flowerheads to be wired up individually, then made into a garland to be placed around the crown of the hat. Once it is finished, keep it cool and out of direct sunlight until you are ready to wear it.

roses

Roses are one of the earliest cultivated flowers. In Roman times they stood for intrigue and celebration. It is said that the Emperor Nero's extravagance with roses was one of the causes of the collapse of the Roman empire. Nowadays, roses—especially red ones—are usually associated with romance. In summer, I love giving and receiving bunches of garden roses, and when I am designing a garden, I always try to include some, preferably shrub roses, whose large blooms add great strength to any border. My favorites are 'Buff Beauty' and 'Felicia.' The mauve-purple foliage of R*osa glauca* syn. *R. rubrifolia* is another must for any garden.

'Margaret Merril' roses and the green spray rose, *R. x odorata* 'Viridiflora' are so special that they do not need any accompaniment. Here I grouped a whole mass of them together without any foliage and placed them in a very simple, rectangular frosted vase. I hope this conveys the idea of a traditional English rose garden at the height of summer.

What could be simpler, yet more elegant and opulent, than this mass of lovely pinkish-white, heavenly scented 'Heritage' garden roses. Artlessly arranged in an old cut-glass container, they look classic on a marble-topped cabinet, with a statuette and the cloud print.

Acknowledgments

Putting this book together has been such a lovely experience. Without such a strong team to help, none of it would have been possible. First, a big, heartfelt thank-you to Lorry Eason, who has taken all the brilliant pictures and who was the most calming influence on me on shoot days. I think you will agree that her photographs have a wonderful depth and magic. Second, thank-you to Françoise Dietrich, the most wonderful art director and designer, who happens to share my passion for food. She helped me choose many of the locations and came to understand my love of flowers. Thanks to her, the pages of this book have been put together in a unique and original way. The award for patience and understanding has to go to Hilary Mandleberg, the editor, without whom the book would not have had any words, nor would it have met the deadline. Thanks, too, to the team at Quadrille, especially Jane O'Shea, whose encouragement and support made this book happen.

I would also like to thank all my family, friends, colleagues, and clients, who have given me so much encouragement and help during the twelve months we were putting this book together. These include Chrissie Rouffignac, Keith Brymer Jones, Mark Watty, and Rosbie Morton. Thanks also to Emma Townsend and Dierdre Taylor, my P.A.s, who made sure I turned up on time and at the right place, and to Heather Alexander who covered for me at work whenever it was necessary.

At Covent Garden Market I would like to thank Alan Gardiner and all his team at Alagar; Dennis, Ted, Andy, and John Painter at Page Monro; Bob Palmer and Charlie French and their team of porters at A. W. Carey; Barry, with his endless selection of foliage at Ronald Porter; David and John Egan for their continued support; Dennis Edwards at David Austin; Terry Dicker and Martin Punter at Arnott & Mason; Craig Broadley and Dave Knight at Quality Plants; Reg Wisbey at Something Special; C. Best and J. Ray and all the team at Evergreen.

Publishers' acknowledgments

The publishers would like to thank the following for the use of their homes: Robert Dye and Lucinda Sebag-Montefiore, whose home was designed by Robert Dye Associates, pages 40–41, 113, 118–19, 129; Mary Evans, pages 16 (left), 17, 68–9, 104–5; Richard Fyfe, pages 16 (center), 54–5, 98–9, 111, 130–31, 141 (bottom); Lawrence Isaacson, interior design by Peter Leonard, pages 18, 66–7, 74–5, 76–7, 82, 136–7; Nik Randall, Suszi Corio, and Louis, whose home was designed by Brookes Stacey Randall, pages 44–5, 78, 85, 93, 94–5, 109, 112, 128; Andrew and Marie Sorrell, pages 15 (bottom), 16 (right), 19 (left), 42, 43, 48–9, 50–51, 52–3, 91, 100–101, 106–7, 120–21, 124–5, 126–7, 140, 141 (top); and Libby Sellors, pages 38 (center), 47, 70–71, 108. They would also like to thank Owain George for the loan of the chair (page 97), William Yeoward for the loan of the vase (page 47), Fianne Stanford from Kirker Greer Candles for the loan of the candles (pages 44–5), Geoff Wilkinson for the cover photograph of the author, Eleanor van Zandt for overseeing the editing of the American edition, John Elsley for his help with the American plant names, and Maggi McCormick for editorial assistance.

Index

INTRODUCTION

In this book you will meet 50 of the oddest animals that live in the sea. Many of them have been discovered by scientists so recently that they have no definite scientific name. Even fewer have a specific common name. Weird creatures ought to get noticed and named. But common names are given to creatures commonly encountered. If an animal lives deep in the sea and manages to avoid capture, then it can carry on indefinitely, keeping its identity secret. If a picture is worth a thousand words, then, for sure, each photo of these 50 weird sea creatures deserves a thousand names.

What makes these creatures odd or weird? More than anything, it is the environment in which they live in the deep ocean — the peculiar conditions to which they've adapted. These include intense pressure far beyond our imagination, and lack of light. In fact, 99% of the sun's light does not permeate below the topmost 330 feet (100 m) of the surface of the sea.

This cast of odd creatures and their deep-sea habitats might seem as far away and improbable as life on Mars. Yet many of them live almost within touching distance in the sense that if you live on the coast or are on a beach vacation or have ever traveled on a cruise ship or ferry, certain deep-sea animals in this book can be found no more than a mile or two away from you. From a ship at sea, for example, grabbing hold of a weight belt or an anchor and taking a deep breath, you could be down among the big-eyed squid and flashing bioluminescent fish in 20 minutes. The problem, of course, even with scuba gear, is that you would not be alive when you finally got near them.

The intense pressure would kill you. It is possible to go very deep in a submarine, but few submarines travel below the upper layers of the ocean. Submarine time for deep-sea-going vessels, even if you can get it, costs the equivalent of King Neptune's ransom.

There have been only two manned voyages to the deepest part of the sea. The deepest spot is the Mariana Trench in the Pacific Ocean, which at 36,000 feet (11,000 m) is 6,500 feet (2,000 m) deeper than Mount Everest is high. The first Mariana Trench voyage took place in the bathyscaphe *Trieste* in 1960, when Don Walsh and Jacques Piccard were lowered to the bottom for a few minutes before concerns about their underwater craft forced them to come back up. In March 2012, *Titanic* director James Cameron climbed into a sub to make the journey, documenting everything he saw for National Geographic.

Two manned voyages to the deepest part of the sea is fewer than the number of manned voyages to the moon (six) and just two more than to Mars (zero), but the fact that they are even on the same scale is astonishing. For us air-breathing, land-loving creatures, the deep sea is impenetrable.

The pressure at 3,280 feet (1 km), where no light penetrates and where some deep-sea creatures live, is 100 times greater than the pressure we feel at the surface. At a depth of 7 miles (11 km), at the bottom, the pressure is 1,100 times that on the surface, or more than 2 tons per square inch. That's the weight of so many miles of water pressing down.

We humans are superbly adapted for life on land, life at sea level. Champion pearl and sponge divers, who use no underwater breathing devices, can reach depths of 100 feet (30 m). Experienced scuba divers can reach 245 feet (75 m) and, with special breathing mixtures, up to 490 feet (150 m). This is nothing compared to the feats of various fish and squid. Marine mammals such as sperm whales and beaked whales can make vertical journeys of 1–2 miles (2–3 km) every few hours.

Adding to the intense pressure, the deep sea is cold and unrelentingly dark. Below the top 330 feet (100 m), which is no more than the skin of the sea, only blue light penetrates. The absolute limit of sunlight penetration is 3,280 feet (1 km) — below that is complete darkness. So how do creatures survive intense, changing pressure in such a cold blackness?

The answer can be found in special adaptations, or traits, that enable a wide variety of animals not only to live at great depth but to move between different depths with different amounts of pressure, light and temperature.

The air pressure within an animal must match that of the outside pressure, or there will be damage to the membranes and blood vessels lining the air spaces and a complete breakdown in normal function. Marine mammals solve the problem by collapsing their lungs and reducing the air space. Deep-sea fish, some of which venture to feed in the upper layers at night, solve the problem with special gas bladders. Those that stay at deeper levels have no swim bladder and their muscles are reduced.

The temperature of the deep, though cold by human standards, is arguably much easier to adapt to because it remains fairly constant with few of the extremes experienced on land and in air. At depths below 3,280 feet (1 km), the temperature is a fairly constant 39°F (4°C). Three-quarters of the ocean has a temperature between 32°F and 43°F (0°C and 6°C). At 13,120 feet (4,000 m), the mean depth of the ocean, the temperature hovers around 1 to 2°C. Exceptions include the hot hydrothermal vents with volcanic activity on the seafloor where unique species have adapted to living in temperatures ranging from 140°F (60°C) to an incredible 867°F (464°C).

The deep-sea currents, though constant, are also more moderate than the wind and wave action at the surface. The deep sea has no hurricanes, cyclones, tornadoes or blizzards. The effects from tsunamis are felt along the shallow coastlines of continental shelves, not in the deeper waters. The deep-sea currents are slow moving. The main water mass in the North Atlantic, the North Atlantic Bottom Water, is created off Greenland and Canada then creeps along the bottom, heading south around the tip of South America at such a slow pace that it can take 1,000 years to reach the North Pacific where it finally returns to the surface waters.

The darkness of the deep has inspired creative solutions. Darkness has forced deep-sea animals to come up with two main strategies to find their food and their mates and to communicate with each other. Some creatures, such as whales and dolphins, use sound. Sound pulses called echolocation allow them to pinpoint the location of food and mates, and other sounds, such as calls and whistles, enable them to communicate with each other over distances of tens, or even hundreds, of miles. But most animals in this book have become masters in the use of light-producing organs called photophores as well as pigment cells called chromatophores. The biochemical emission of light is called bioluminescence.

Photophores are light-producing organs that come in a variety of types, purposes and sizes. Some are simple; others are surrounded by reflectors, lenses, light guides, color filters and special muscles that enable them to adjust the color, intensity and direction of the light they produce. Photophores produce light through a chemical reaction.

Chromatophores are pigment cells that change the color of an animal by expanding or contracting. Sometimes located around photophores, they may shield the reflections of the photophore when it's not active. Squid and octopus are masters in the use of chromatophores for camouflage and communication.

Other deep-sea animals, such as the angler fish with its lure, are able to work with bacteria to produce the light they need in the deep.

The language of light in the deep sea is complex and, depending on one's perspective, either dangerous or beautiful. Pretending we are on board a deep-sea-going submarine with clear portholes, we would gaze out in wonder. Some fish, as they swim by, appear to be carrying lanterns, their bodies only faintly visible in the gloom. The light is at the tip of a stalk sticking up from their forehead or hanging down from their chin. Another smaller fish, flashing fiery

red and blue signals from its sides, in some techno beat pattern, swims toward the lantern, mouth open. A split second later, the smaller fish perhaps senses its mistake as the massive mouth attached to the light on a stalk engulfs it, swallowing it. Instantly, the lights of the prey disappear, every glimmer of light absorbed by the dark gut wall of the predator, the fire extinguished.

Next come the dancing jellyfish and the carnivorous comb jelly (also known as the sea walnut), both of them pulsing in the current, lit up in reds, oranges, yellows and bits of blue. The colors are artificial — refractive colors like the light from a prism or rainbow. They attract prey by looking like an amusement park ride or Vegas sign. They float by as if on parade, the neon messages flashing, then all goes dark. Like all animals they need to communicate in some way with their own kind, but they don't want to signal their location to predators.

After more lantern-carrying fish, we meet the deep-sea dragonfish. And then, looming up from the black, a jewel, or cock-eyed, squid with giant eyes tries to glimpse the light from any of these creatures as it jets by in search of food.

For these and other deep-sea animals, being able to make one's own light has been the key to survival. A few of them have mastered certain special light channels, often red wavelengths, that only animals of their kind can see. Because few animals can see it, the use of red light normally keeps an animal safe below 328 feet (100 m), where no red light penetrates. Those few that can see red clearly have an advantage. The light allows for communication, enables animals to hunt and can help them to avoid predators. Patterns of flashing light can be used for honest communication or for sheer trickery, as with the lantern-carrying fish that give a false impression of their location. Mostly we have no idea to what extent light is used and what message is being transmitted. As with the sounds of whales, the deep-sea world of flashing colored lights is largely a mystery. Humans live their lives on another channel.

Given all the difficulties humans have adapting to deep-sea conditions, how were the state-of-the-art photographs in this book taken?

The possible options might include taking photos through the portholes of submarines, but such portholes are small, fish scatter on the approach of a submarine and powerful lights are needed to see even a few feet into the darkness. Another option might be to lower a camera into the deep, but this would be difficult to operate at the required depth from above the surface, even given knowledge about the day-to-day life and habitat of possible subjects. Combine the logistical problems with the moving fish and squid and the task of getting a clear, well-lit image seems impossible. Even planktonic animals (ones that drift freely) are constantly moving with the currents; fish and squid may dart around. The solution has been to catch and bring the animals to a ship on the surface and then recreate a natural-looking environment in a tank. Nearly all the photos in this book were taken this way.

Collecting in the deep sea is like sampling a pond with a teaspoon. The chances of catching anything are slim. Photographers David Shale, Solvin Zankl and

Jeff Rotman worked with oceanography institutes, museums and the BBC Natural History Unit, taking long cruises to record and to try to understand these little-studied residents of the deep sea. Every day during a cruise, nets and sometimes remote-operated vehicles (ROVs) with cameras and special collecting devices were lowered at various points and to various depths. As soon as the trawl was hauled aboard, the photographers would race to transfer the most unusual animals to fresh seawater aquariums in a chilled laboratory below deck. Sometimes air bubbles or detritus needed to be removed. Most animals were then photographed against a black background using a black velvet screen placed behind the subject. Flash guns on either side of the tank were synchronized to the camera and illuminated the subject against the black background. Once the images were recorded, the photographers did not manipulate them. Shale's stated mission is not only to "catalogue representatives of as many different species as possible, but to present them in the most realistic way."

The most astonishing thing about the deep sea is that these weird sea creatures not only survive the cold, dark, high-pressure conditions, but they flourish. The extent of the diversity of life in the depths is so great as to be simply unknown. Many scientists, however, believe it may rival the most productive and diverse land areas, such as the tropical rainforest.

In 2010 the Census of Marine Life completed its 10-year search for deep-ocean species. This census increased the number of identified marine species by about 1,330, bringing the total number of known marine species to 250,000 with more than 5,000 of these still awaiting formal description. Yet the true number — based on Census of Marine Life findings and a growing body of research into marine life — may one day top one million, or even considerably more, marine species. Each species' successful solution to the problem of how to live and flourish in the deep sea is a result of millions of years of evolution. This means there may be more than one million ways to solve the challenge of how to live in the deep sea and flourish.

As we celebrate weird creatures, keep in mind that weirdness is relative. The ocean comprises more than 90% of the living space on Earth. Even though less than 1% of the ocean has been explored, the ocean, especially the deep ocean, is more typical of our Earth than anywhere on land, such as a forest, a savannah, a city or a shopping mall. These weird creatures are arguably the typical, normal citizens of our planet — much more so than anything found on land.

As you turn the pages and gaze into strange, wild eyes and study these faces with crooked or toothless smiles, you are looking at the fruits of deep-sea evolution. Try to guess what the patterns of lights on their bodies are "saying" and appreciate the artistry of the photographers' work. Take in the wonder, the extraordinary weirdness, of what lives in the seas seemingly close, yet elusive, deep and far away from us.

DEEP-SEA BLACKDEVIL ANGLER FISH

(*Melanocetus murrayi*)

Also known as the deep-sea blackdevil, or Murray's abyssal angler fish, this species usually lives at depths of 3,280 to 8,200 feet (1,000 to 2,500 m), but it has been found at more than 19,685 feet (6,000 m) below the surface. The fleshy "fishing pole" growing from above its mouth is covered in bioluminescent bacteria (a bacteria that produces light) that attracts prey in the darkness. Pictured is the female, which grows up to a size of 4¾ inches (12 cm). The male reaches a length of only ¾ inch (2 cm) and lives as a parasite, attached to the female. It's a permanent arrangement — till death do they part.

WAVY CLIO

(Clio recurva)
The wavy clio, also sometimes called the
deep-sea butterfly, is a sea snail that floats
free in the water. It belongs to the group of
pteropods called Opisthobranchia, which
means that the gills are situated behind
the heart. Wavy clios range in size from
¼ inch (0.5 cm) to ½ inch (1.3 cm).

SEA SNAIL

(Atlanta peroni)
This carnivorous snail lives in the upper 1,640 feet (500 m) of the ocean, where it undertakes daily vertical migrations to prey on zooplankton. It has large, movable, complex eyes and only one lobed foot, which is a flattened fin with a keel that it uses for swimming. The thin coiled shell is so transparent that the interior organs can be seen.

JEWEL SQUID, OR COCK-EYED SQUID (left)

(*Histioteuthis bonellii*)

Found living at 610 to 1,663 feet (186 to 507 m) depths in waters above the Mid-Atlantic Ridge, which runs south from Iceland, this 3-foot (1 m) squid can often be seen lit up like a Christmas tree. The pattern of photophores, which are the specialized organs that emit a light called bioluminescence, helps to make this squid look like it has a bad case of measles. It also has chromatophores, which are pigment cells that can expand and contract to absorb light to change the color of the body. Other photophores direct light down in the water as camouflage. Its different-size eyes are adapted to the gloomy depths. One huge eye points up, catching light from the surface to search for predators and prey. The small eye searches for predators, prey and mates, checking for the bioluminescent flashes from other animals that swim by.

PIGLET SQUID (above)

(*Helicocranchia pfefferi*)

Many deep-sea animals migrate daily from deep waters to the surface. With a face like the character in Winnie the Pooh, the small, transparent piglet squid is born in the upper layers of the ocean and moves ever deeper as it develops and ages. This could be called "developmental migration." In this photo, an immature piglet squid displays, just below its short arms, the large funnel that sticks out and will be used to push itself forward. A squid's funnel is like a jet engine. When escaping from a predator, a piglet squid can move itself as fast as 25 body lengths a second.

YETI CRAB (above)

(unnamed; *Kiwa* sp.)

The yeti crab, so called because of its hairy undersides, lives only around deep-sea hydrothermal vents (which are openings in the seafloor from which hot water gushes out). This probable new species was found on the Dragon Hydrothermal Vent Field in the tropical southeast Indian Ocean in November 2011. Yeti crabs are known to collect a type of bacteria called chemosynthetic bacteria on their hairy bottoms, and it is thought that they can harvest these bacteria as a food source.

DEEP-SEA BARRACUDA (right)

(unnamed; *Sphyraena* sp.)

The deep-sea barracuda opens its mouth wide, a three-fang predator smile. It was found at a depth of 1,640 feet (500 m) off Eilat, Israel, in the Red Sea. Barracudas, with their characteristic long bodies, are found in tropical and subtropical waters at various depths.

DEEP-SEA OPOSSUM SHRIMP (above)

(*Gnathophausia ingens*)
This deep-water shrimp is 5 to 20 times the size of the familiar coastal shrimp. A giant of the deep, it reaches lengths of up to 14 inches (35 cm), though it is usually smaller. Red animals only appear red if they are reflecting light. In the deep, where there is usually no red light, they are invisible, giving them an edge for hunting as well as avoiding predators. Of course, its larger body also helps it overwhelm prey and probably means it produces larger or more numerous eggs.

SCALY-FOOT GASTROPOD OR SEA SNAIL (right)

(unidentified new species)
This sea snail was first spotted at the Dragon Hydrothermal Vent Field in the tropical southeast Indian Ocean in November 2011. It lives side by side with yeti crabs on the hydrothermal vent chimneys, tolerant of the hot water and hydrogen sulfide pouring out of cracks in the volcanic seafloor. Of note is the foot of the snail, which in most species is exposed, but this species has armor-like scales that may protect it from the hot water as well as from predators. Like so many finds in the deep ocean, scientists can tell you it resembles known species but have yet to name and formally describe it. A type of worm, called polychaete worms, are attached to the snail and live on it.

PRAM BUG (right)

(*Phronima sedentaria*)

This 1-inch (2.5 cm) long shrimp-like amphipod inspired the design for the monster in the movie *Alien*. It is all arms and legs, including big claws and two sets of eyes to hunt prey. The mothers-to-be attack and devour the insides of the salp, taking over the dead animal's barrel-like shell as a kind of baby stroller (what the British call a pram). She lays her eggs and raises her young in the shell, and she uses it as a vehicle to hunt for more prey.

SOLITARY SALP (below)

(*Iasis zonaria*)

Solitary salps are not always solitary. They alternate generations. During the solitary salp phase, it floats alone in the deep North Atlantic, sometimes swimming by jet propulsion (movement by sucking in water and blowing it out). It reproduces asexually (no partner needed to produce young), forming a long chain and living together in colonies when food is abundant. Its gelatinous outer tunic is protective — until an animal such as the dangerous shrimp-like pram bug invades and eats it alive from the inside, all but the shell, which it recycles as its own nest. Salps filter-feed, passing water containing plant and animal plankton into the cavity, where it is filtered as it passes through and out the gut.

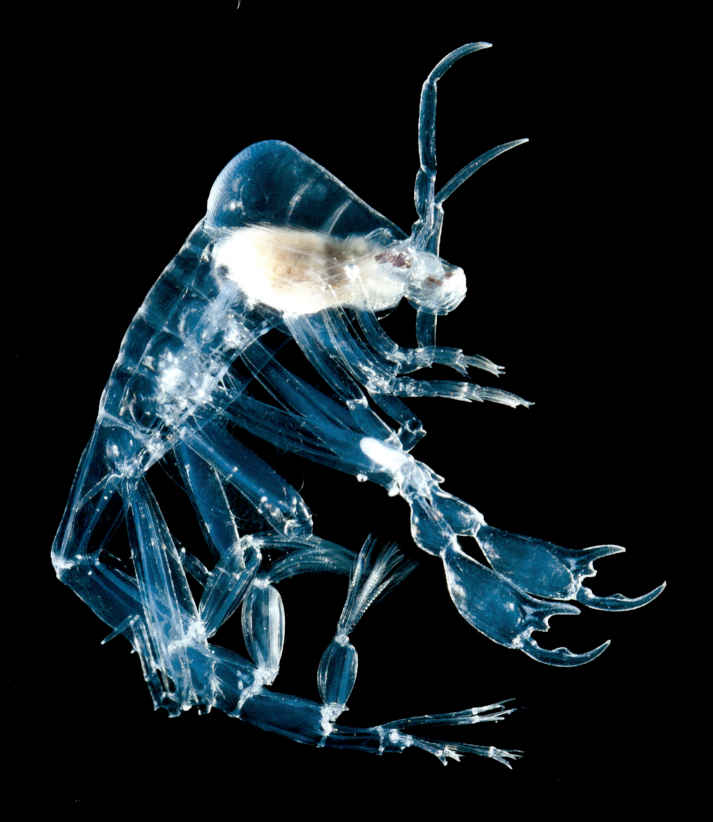

DEEP-SEA SHRIMP

(no common or species name; *Pasiphaea* sp.)
This nameless female deep-sea shrimp — her eyes ever
watchful for predators — carries her eggs until they are
ready to hatch. The colors of shrimp species vary from
transparent near the surface to deep orange or even
bright red in the deepest layers of the ocean. In both
cases color, or lack of it, provides camouflage. Deep-sea
shrimp that migrate up and down in the water column
are often half red and half transparent. This female,
found in the dark mesopelagic zone between 1,750 and
2,460 feet (530 and 750 m) deep in the North Atlantic,
has some color and some transparency.

GLASS SQUID

(*Teuthowenia megalops*)
Also known as the cranchiid squid, it has large eyes and numerous pigment cells called chromatophores covering its transparent body. It lives in the North Atlantic, where it is usually found below 3,300 feet (1,000 m). The completely transparent juveniles live closer to the surface.

HYDROMEDUSAN JELLYFISH

(*Crossota millsae*)

This dangerously beautiful jellyfish drifts along the seafloor trailing its tentacles to catch prey — which is whatever might come into contact with it. On contact, its stinging cells, or nematocysts, shoot toxin into the prey. This jellyfish was found on the Mid-Atlantic Ridge, 8,860 feet (2,700 m) below the surface. The reddish colors provide an extraordinary display yet are invisible to its prey. Jellyfish have no brain or central nervous system, and they rely on a loose network of nerve cells to indicate where and when to move in reaction to possible predators or prey.

FEATHER STAR (below)

(unidentified species)
A relative of starfish and sea urchins, this suspected new species of feather star has a typical pose: It uses some of its stiff yet flexible arms to hold on to the ocean floor while it raises its other arms into the current to try to catch and gather passing particles of food. If the feeding is poor, they sometimes let go of the seafloor and swim along by swinging their arms around — a graceful deep-sea ballet. This marine invertebrate was found only in December 2011 and has yet to be formally named.

FANGTOOTH (right)

(*Anoplogaster cornuta*)
Lurking above the Mid-Atlantic Ridge, the up to 7 inches (18 cm) long fangtooth bares its sharp teeth. In fact, the teeth are impossible to disguise; the only question is how wide its mouth can open — up to about 180 degrees. This predator is found between 1,640 and 16,400 feet (500 and 5,000 m) below the surface of the ocean, but the adults reside in the more productive upper layers, from 1,640 to 6,560 feet (500–2,000 m), where they catch fish and squid. The young stay deep — safe from hungry tuna and other predators.

SPINED PYGMY SHARK (below)

(*Squaliolus laticaudus*)
Thought to be the world's smallest shark, measuring only up to 10 inches (25 cm) for females and 9 inches (23 cm) for males, the spined pygmy shark lives at depths of 650 to 6,500 feet (200 to 2,000 m) in tropical waters over the continental slopes. It makes vertical migrations, meaning it swims up and down in the water depending on the time of day, using the luminous photophores (special organs that produce light) on its underside to blend in with the surface and be less visible to predators. Despite its looks, it is not dangerous to humans.

ANTHOMEDUSAN JELLYFISH (right)

(*Pandea rubra*)
Also known as the red paper lantern jellyfish, the name "anthomedusan" means the "flower jellyfish." Whether paper lantern or flower, both names attempt to describe an odd beauty. Living in the deep Gulf of Maine, off northeastern U.S. and Canada, the special structure of this jellyfish, or sea jelly, allows it to fold vertically and compress along what appear to be folds under its umbrella (also called the bell, due to the shape). Jellyfish have no eyes, but some jellyfish have light-sensitive organs called ocelli.

SNIPE EEL (above)

(*Nemichthys scolopaceus*)
When outstretched to its full 16 inches (40 cm) and hanging vertically in the water, the snipe eel is in its typical hunting posture. Note the wide-open jaws, specialized to stay open, which enable it to snare careless shrimp. When the prey's antennae get tangled up in the teeth, the snipe eel secures its catch and then swallows it.

BLACK DRAGONFISH (right)

(*Melanostomias melanops*)
The black dragonfish has no scales and is a slender, up to 12-inch (30 cm) long deep-sea fish. The fleshy part growing from its chin lures curious prey close enough for the dragonfish to seize it in its toothy mouth. Light-emitting organs along the lower part of its body and below its eye help it avoid predators through what is called deceptive illumination. This species can be found between 1,640 and 2,600 feet (500 and 800 m) deep in the Atlantic, Indian and Pacific Oceans.

HYPERIID AMPHIPOD (above)

(no common name; *Scypholanceola stephensi*)
This animal is a kind of hyperiid amphipod — part of
the order of soft-bodied crustaceans that includes sand
hoppers and sand fleas. It lives in saltwater and has
been found at depths of up to 29,500 feet (9,000 m). It
likes to hitchhike on the outside of the bell of jellyfish.
It feeds on small planktonic animals such as copepods.
Its deep orange color gives it camouflage in the "red
channel" of the deep sea, where few species can see it.

MAUVE STINGER (right)

(*Pelagia noctiluca*)
This medusa, or jellyfish, occurs sometimes in great
numbers at the surface. It is found in the warm
temperate waters of the world's oceans. It produces
light called bioluminescence, which attracts its food. It
feeds on smaller creatures called zooplankton, which it
catches with its tentacles, using its poisonous stinging
cells. In an unprecedented event on November 21,
2007, an invading 10-square-mile (26 km^2) swarm
of billions of these jellyfish wiped out a 100,000-fish
salmon farm in Northern Ireland, causing over
$1 million in damages.

NAKED SEA BUTTERFLY

(*Clione limacina*)
These semi-transparent gastropods, also known as sea
angels, swim through cold, deep waters using their two
fleshy paddles, which are a modification of the foot of
a snail. They might be described as "lovely but lethal" to
other small shelled sea snails — their specialized prey.

SEA CUCUMBER

(no common name; *Peniagone diaphana*)
Most sea cucumbers can only crawl slowly along the
sea bottom. This one not only crawls but is an active
swimmer when it needs to move to new feeding areas.
Its see-through body reveals the simplicity of the sea
cucumber body plan: a simple gut passing through
the center of the body with, at either end, a mouth and
an anus. Sea cucumbers, also known as holothurians,
eat like earthworms. They gulp the soft sediment from
the bottom and sift it through their body for nutrients,
expelling what they don't need. Their key ecological role
is to recycle the seafloor's sediments.

SLOANE'S VIPERFISH

(*Chauliodus sloani*)

Viperfish belong to the deep-sea fish order of toothy dragonfish found in waters up to 3,280 feet (1,000 m) deep. The pattern of photophores (the light-producing organs) on their bodies emits bioluminescence and gives them a spooky glow. The lights flash in complex patterns, and they may allow viperfish to communicate with each other, or the fish may use them to lure, trick and/or illuminate their prey, or even to confuse potential predators.

BOBTAIL SQUID

(*Rossia* sp.)

The bobtail squid, related to cuttlefish, lives on the bottom of the sea. It has eight arms, each with suckers at the ends, plus two longer tentacles, typical of squid. It uses small fins at the back of its body to swim just above the bottom of the ocean. When chased or cornered by predators it can also resort to jet propulsion, squirting out a cloud of black ink as it pumps water through its body to move itself forward.

PACIFIC HATCHET FISH

(Argyropelecus affinis)

What might a hatchet fish see if it looked at its reflection? Living in the twilight world at depths of 985 to 2,100 feet (300 to 650 m), it cannot see much, but its huge eyes take in as much light as possible, which helps it avoid predators. On its underside, to protect it from being seen from below, the Pacific hatchet fish has organs called photophores that emit blue light, which masks the fish against the faint light of the surface. Hunting under the cover of night to avoid predators, hatchet fish swim to higher depths to feed on plankton.

DEEP-SEA DRAGONFISH (left)

(*Aristostomias* sp.)
As if lit by a Hollywood horror film director, this profile of a deep-sea dragonfish reveals the combination of white and red light that it uses to hunt red-bodied crustaceans in the dark, deep sea. It is also known as the loosejaw fish, referring to its flexible lower jaw, which it can extend forward and appears to be hinged.

DEEP-SEA URCHIN (right)

(unidentified species)
Similar to the sea urchins found in shallow waters, this deep-sea version lives on the seafloor of the Indian Ocean. Moving around on tiny tube feet, it searches for decaying animal parts that drift down from the surface. A sea urchin's mouth is in the middle of the underside of its body. When it finds a piece of food, it uses suckers on the ends of its feet to grab the piece of food, and its teeth scrape away a section so it can jam the tiny pieces into its mouth. Many species of these "porcupines of the seafloor" are armed with poisonous spines.

ROUND RAY

(*Rajella fyllae*)

The juvenile round ray is a bottom-living fish found at depths ranging from 560 to 6,725 feet (170 to 2,050 m). It grows up to 22 inches (55 cm) long and lives in the northern North Atlantic and nearby waters. Its back is rough and covered with tiny thorns, especially on its head. It also has prickles on its fins as well as several rows of midline thorns. The arrangement of these thorns changes depending on the sex and age of the ray. The round ray has 30 to 38 rows of teeth in its upper jaw. These teeth are blunt, conical and cusped (meaning they have sections that stick out, like we do on our molar teeth), perfect for eating small crustaceans and mollusks. This individual was found living on the bottom of the cold Barents Sea, off Norway.

DEEP-SEA ANEMONE

(unidentified species)

Deep-sea anemones look to most of the world like the flowers of the sea. Perhaps this is their disguise. These invertebrates (animals without a backbone) are predators with tentacles equipped with stinging cells. They use their tentacles to defend themselves and to capture prey, such as small fish and shrimp. Each stinging cell has a sensory hair that, when touched, mechanically triggers the cell explosion, which is a harpoon-like structure that attaches to the flesh of the aggressor or prey and injects a dose of poison. The poison is a mix of toxins, including neurotoxins that paralyze the prey and allow the anemone to move it to its mouth for digestion. Found throughout the world's oceans and at various depths, anemones are related to corals and jellyfish. Anemones attach themselves to the sea bottom with an adhesive foot and tend to stay in the same spot until food runs out or a predator attacks. Then the anemones release themselves and use flexing motions to swim to a new location. This anemone was found on the Coral Seamount in the tropical southeast Indian Ocean.

MESOPELAGIC COPEPOD (above)

(no common name; *Gaussia princeps*)
Compared to the average copepod length of ¹⁄₂₄ to ¹⁄₁₂ inch (1 to 2 mm), this copepod is gigantic, measuring up to 1 inch (27 mm long). Copepods make up some 60 percent of the sea's marine plankton. Copepods contribute to the light show in the sea with bioluminescent effects that include their favorite escape method: waving their antennae and producing a bright cloud of light when they flee, confusing predators. Still, it doesn't always work, as copepods are a main food in the sea for everything from small fish to giant whales.

DUMBO, THE OCTOPOD (right)

(*Grimpoteuthis discoveryi*)
Called "Dumbo" because the fins make it look like the Disney cartoon flying elephant, this octopod has webbed arms that extend almost to the tips and sensitive tentacles equipped with small cirri (very thin appendages) along each side of the suckers. A big-eyed animal, it lives along the bottom of the Mid-Atlantic Ridge, its orangish coloring making it invisible.

ATLANTIC LONGARM OCTOPUS

(*Octopus defilippi*)

The larval form of the Atlantic longarm octopus shows the early development of the eyes, arms and a few of the pigment cells called chromatophores. When fully grown, this octopus will be 3 feet (1 m) long, 85 to 90 percent of which will be arms. The entire body of the adult will be covered in chromatophores, the pigmented cells enabling it to change its color.

NORTHERN STOPLIGHT LOOSEJAW

(*Malacosteus niger*)

The northern stoplight loosejaw mainly preys on copepods. This species is in the small club of deep-sea fish able to emit and see red light. The northern stoplight loosejaw shines the red light on its prey, but predators and competitors can't see the predator or the prey. The prey doesn't even notice that it is in the spotlight — until it's too late.

CALANOID COPEPOD (above)

(no common name; *Valdiviella* sp.)
These two female copepods, each about ⅙ inch (5 mm) long, are carrying egg sacs attached to their abdomen. Deep-sea copepods are often red in color, which makes them invisible to most predators in the depths. Although they are mainly planktonic, meaning they float freely on ocean currents, they do have long antennae that they can use to strike backward along their sides, allowing them to advance through the water. With some 14,000 species of copepods, they are the most diverse group of crustaceans.

ORANGEBACK FLYING SQUID (right)

(*Sthenoteuthis pteropus*)
This squid mainly lives in the upper 650 feet (200 m), but it can swim as deep as 5,000 feet (1,500 m). Adults can grow to be more than 6 feet (2 m) long including the tentacles. The name "pteropus" is from the Greek "ptero," meaning wing, named after the pair of muscular fins at the tip of its mantle (its main body), which it uses to move. It is also known to break through the surface of the water, flying through the air momentarily before zooming back down to the depths. The many small photophores under the skin of the mantle, head and arms are grouped together to form a large, oval luminous spot on the back. It lives in the tropical and subtropical North Atlantic Ocean.

AMPHIPOD (no common name; *Epimeria cornigera*)

with LOPHELIA COLD-WATER CORAL (*Lophelia pertusa*)

This crustacean in the order Amphipoda does not have a common name. It lives at depths of more than a thousand feet (several hundred meters), such as above the cold-water reefs off the Norwegian coast, where it was found on this white Lophelia coral. Distributed throughout the northeast Atlantic, this crustacean has a maximum body length of approximately ⅝ inch (16 mm) and feeds on hydroids, which are tiny creatures related to jellyfish.

DEEP-SEA BRITTLE STAR

(unidentified species, class *Ophiuroidea*)
Closely related to starfish and sea urchins, deep-sea brittle stars are members of an ancient group of animals called Echinodermata. They live on the seabed, sometimes thousands of them together, each one raising its five arms to try to capture drifting particles of food — tiny plankton and other nutrients pushed along by deep-sea currents.

SOUTHERN PURPLE ENTEROPNEUST, or ACORN WORM

(Yoda purpurata)
This new species — found in 2010, 12,140 feet (3,700 m) below the ocean's surface above the Mid-Atlantic Ridge — is a member of a group that may be the evolutionary link between vertebrate (with a backbone) and invertebrate (without a backbone) animals. It has the head, tail and basic body plan of a backboned animal but no brain, eyes or known sense organs. It feeds on sediment on the seafloor, leaving behind a distinctive spiral trail.

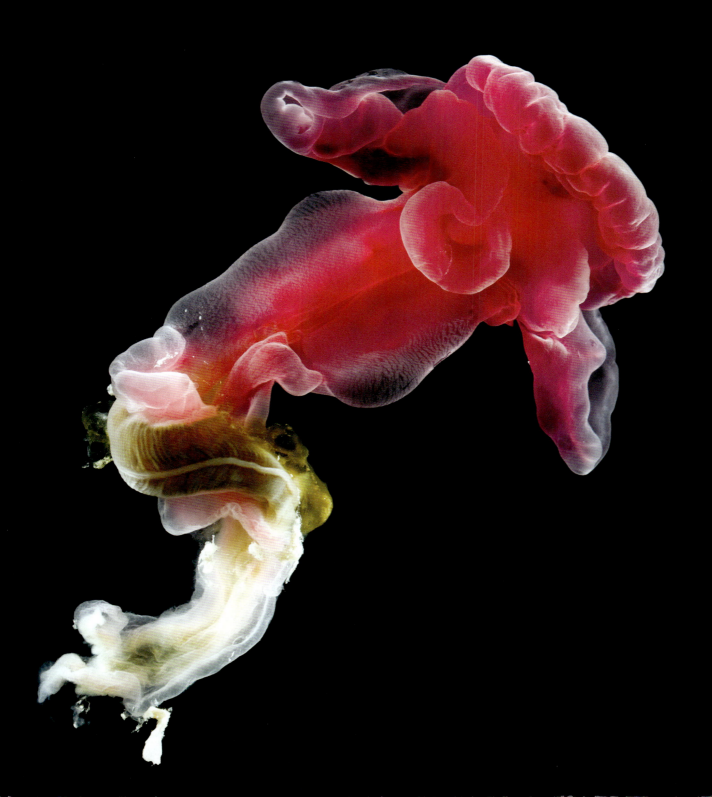

BENTHIC OCTOPUS

(*Benthoctopus johnstoniana*)

This deep-sea bottom-dwelling octopus was found living on the Mid-Atlantic Ridge. Most marine species are pale on the underside and dark on top. This gives them camouflage for hunting or avoiding predators. Animals above may not see the dark shape below them, while from below they usually fail to notice the light side, which blends in with the upper layers of the ocean. But the benthic octopus shows reverse counter-shading, being paler on top than on bottom. There are at least 25 different species of benthic octopus living in the sea between 650 and 9,800 feet (200 and 3,000 m) deep.

SEA SPIDER

(*Colossendeis* sp.)

Sea spiders, unrelated to land-based spiders, are common crawlers along the bottom of the deep seafloor. Each of their long, jointed legs ends in a sharp claw. The claws allow them to grab the bottom even in strong currents, and they are their main food-gathering tool. They eat anemones, soft corals and other sedentary or slow-moving animals. They use their proboscis to explore the tissues of their prey and suck them out of their shells.

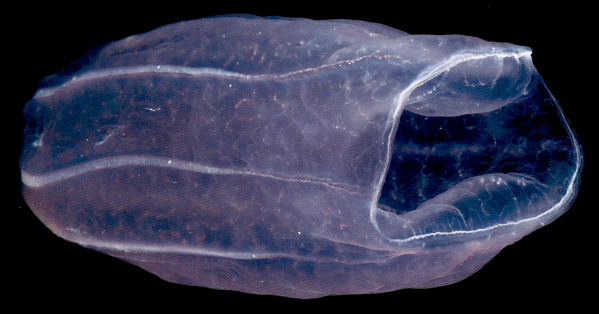

COMB JELLY

(Beroe cucumis)

The always hungry comb jelly (or sea walnut), a ctenophore, might be described as little more than a mouth that swims. Using its rows of comb plates along the sides of its body, the comb jelly swims through the water. Like squid it is also capable of a type of jet propulsion, squirting water from its mouth end to jet around. That mouth is used to prey on other comb jellies, which it swallows whole.

SQUAT LOBSTER

(*Galathea* sp. *or Munida* sp.)

The squat lobster, also known as the galatheid crab, is mostly a bottom-dwelling scavenger. It is found worldwide and at various depths. It congregates in great numbers, scrapping for food around the oasis-like hydrothermal vents. Some squat lobsters living in burrows in deep waters off Scotland have been observed using their extraordinarily long arms and pincers to catch northern krill.

SEA CUCUMBER (above)

(no common name; *Deima validum*)
This sea cucumber was found on the Mid-Atlantic Ridge, some 8,200 feet (2,500 m) down in the North Atlantic. As with other sea cucumbers living in shallow waters, it has a stiff body structure and skin that shows many spicules (which are small, needle-like structures), giving it a rough texture.

DEEP-SEA LARVAL CRAB (right)

(unknown species)
What looks part crab, part lobster and part Sesame Street muppet? Crabs go through various stages of development. The final larval stage, before the crab molts (sheds its shell) and becomes a juvenile crab, is called the megalopa form. It lasts only a week. Megalopa crabs are unable to swim. They are carried by currents, and the lucky ones drift through thick zooplankton patches where they eat as much as they can.

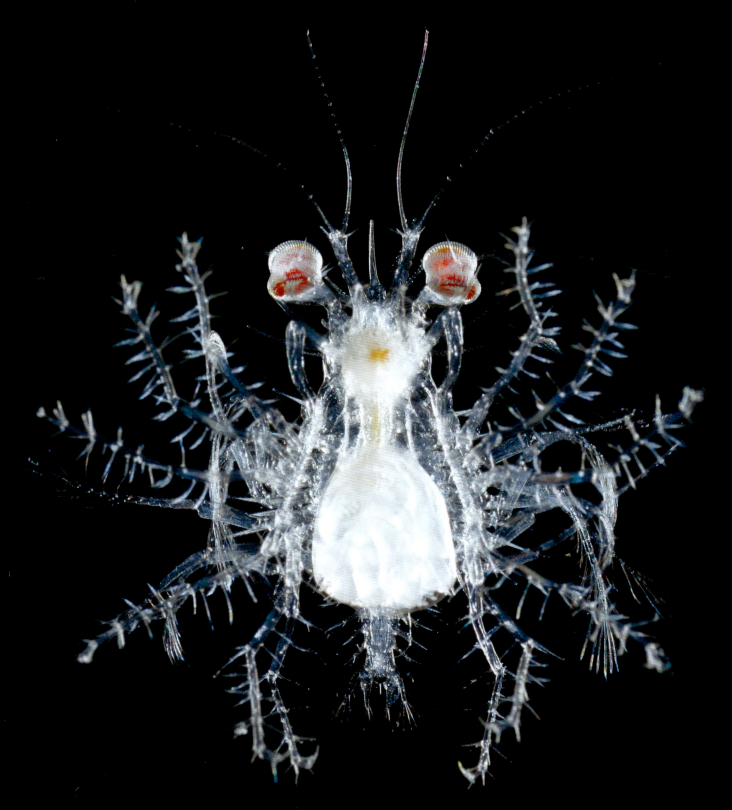

MANTIS SHRIMP LARVA

(Order Stomatopoda; species cannot be identified from larval stage)

The mantis shrimp is a lightning-fast predator that has among the most complex eyes in the animal kingdom. It is able to read even ultraviolet and polarized light. The larvae are frightening and prey on other larval forms, while remaining largely camouflaged in the phytoplankton (due to their transparent bodies). As adults, they will acquire red, green, blue and flashing fluorescent yellow colors and move into excavated burrows or rock crevices, as their eyes, set on stalks, survey the passing food parade. When they see an appealing fish, or shellfish, their powerful limbs uncork, spearing or clubbing the prey, delivering a blow at 33 feet (10 m) per second, equivalent to the force of a 22-caliber bullet. Some species of mantis shrimps are highly promiscuous (meaning they have several mates) and others mate for life, one pairing lasting 20 years.

OIKOPLEURA SEA SQUIRT

(*Oikopleura* sp.)

Oikopleura is a type of sea squirt, or tunicate, called a larvacean, meaning that it stays in the larval form even as an adult. This one, only ¹⁄₂₄ inch (1 mm) long, resembles a tadpole with a translucent rainbow-colored tail. Vertebrates may have evolved from larvacean-like animals. Found in all oceans, sea squirts are tunicates without tunics. Instead, they make secret gelatinous containers that provide them with temporary shelter and allow them to filter water to get their food. Their lives are short: five to ten days. They spend most of their time building and rebuilding these containers, which last perhaps only a couple hours, and feeding as much as possible.

SEA CUCUMBER

(*Amperima* sp.)

If you could walk on the deep seafloor, you would meet many of these sea cucumbers, or holothurians. This one was found 8,200 feet (2,500 m) down in the North Atlantic. Sea cucumbers take their nutrition from the loose particles that drift down from the surface and cover the bottom of the sea. This recycling process is similar to the work done by earthworms to recycle soil. Sea cucumbers generally move slowly, but some species can lift off the ocean floor and swim or ride the currents to move to new feeding areas.

THREE-SPINED CAVOLINE (right)

(*Diacria trispinosa*)

This ⅜-inch (1 cm) long sea snail has a foot that forms into two wing-like structures used for swimming. It feeds on plant plankton in the upper layers of the ocean, and it is known to create mucous nets to harvest the phytoplankton. The plankton sticks to the nets and is then collected and eaten by the three-spined cavoline. Found at a depth of 650 to 1,640 feet (200–500 m), this one was trailing an egg string.

INDEX